A Philistine's Journal

An Average Guy Tackles the Classics

WT

6/8/03

By Wayne Turmel

New Leaf ✧ Illinois

A New Leaf Book
Published by WigWam Publishing Co.
P.O. Box 6992
Villa Park, IL 60181
http://www.newleafbooks.net

Cover art illustration by Frank K. Krug

Printed in the U.S.A.

To Roger and Walline
For the great gifts of wanderlust and words

A Philistine's Journal

An Average Guy Tackles the Classics

By Wayne Turmel

Table of Contents

INTRODUCTION

Lordy, Lordy, Look Who's Forty

When my mother turned forty, the Fraser Valley Record (the *New York Times* of Mission, BC) ran an ad in the classified section with a picture of her as a teenager and the bold type, "Lordy, Lordy, Look Who's Forty— Happy Birthday Walline."

Turning forty was a very big deal in the Turmel household. I know this because

1. it was an occasion for poetry (Hey, it rhymed—more or less) and;
2. no one in our family, particularly my Aunt Heather, was going to waste good money on something that didn't really matter. Remember, this is a woman who took to disciplining her kids with a plastic spatula after breaking a wooden spoon over my cousin David's behind. She felt no remorse for the whupping, but that was a $2 spoon and she wasn't going to take the chance of breaking another one.

Nope, springing for a picture ad, even in our rinky-dink local rag was not to be sniffed at.

Now here I was, twenty-two years later, staring forty in the eye. No ad in the paper, no party—we only moved to Chicago a month ago and still don't know anyone I don't share a boss with—and not feeling much like celebrating anyway.

1

What in the Wide, Wide World of Sports[1] was wrong with me? Physically I was fine. I had just undergone my annual physical that said so. Any man who has experienced his first prostate exam will testify to its life-altering impact.

Besides determining I was fine, or at least in reasonable shape for the shape I'm in, it also crossed about four requests off my list of sexual things I wanted my wife to let me do to her. Do unto others and all that....

So what was the diagnosis? Let's see:

- Just turned forty
- Living in a new city, in a relatively new country (I'd moved from Canada to Los Angeles ten years prior)
- Married to an amazingly patient, wonderful woman (hereafter known as The Duchess) who had just volunteered to follow me and my paycheck halfway across the country
- One amazing daughter, Her Serene Highness, who generally adores her daddy but wasn't speaking to me in hopes this was all a mistake and we'd move back to California when I came back to my senses
- A house in the suburbs—admittedly a rental, but it's a house, and it is in the suburbs so it qualifies
- A good job where I'm paid decently for a corporate drone position. It's even more astonishing to think that I have very little college education and none of the usual business experience. Still, I've survived three mergers and buyouts in the last five years and am headed for number four, but the checks keep coming and life is good
- A reputation for being a pretty good guy. Fun at parties

---

1. Yes, that is a *Blazing Saddles* reference. Bonus points for knowing it was Slim Pickens who said it. If the notion of Mel Brooks and Plutarch in the same volume strikes you as too much to handle, put down the book right now, walk away, and no one gets hurt.

and kind to dogs and old ladies. I've even woken up to find myself attending church again, after a twenty-year hiatus

What we have here, methinks, is a classic case of mid-life crisis. Regardless of what the doctors say, forty is indeed mid-life, at least for a Turmel. There are goldfish that outlive my kinfolk.

So let's assume I've earned it. What kind of crisis should I have? I'd love nothing more than to just start home from work one day, head south on Rt. 53 and keep going till I need a passport, like the guy in that Steve Earle song, "The Week of Living Dangerously,"[2] but I can't bring myself to do it. It wouldn't be right, and I'm generally about doing what's right (whether I succeed or not is another issue entirely) as opposed to what's smart. I know there's a big long philosophical name for someone who more or less accepts life as it's presented to him, but for the life of me I can't think of it right now.

The list of things I don't know is fairly impressive. Yes, I know a lot of trivia, which passes for knowledge. Heck, I've even been on *Jeopardy* (although I wound up with $0 and suffered a humiliating defeat of Dukakis-like proportions) which impresses people to some degree, but I don't pretend to know much that actually matters. God, religion (don't tell me they're the same thing, I'm not buying it), politics beyond the front page, philosophy, poetry, literature going back further than Robert Ludlum—it's all pretty much a big egg-sucking mystery to me.

One of the things that The Duchess loves about me, even if she can't relate, is that I take it very personally that I will probably shuffle off this mortal coil before knowing everything. It doesn't stop me from trying though.

Boy, this mid-life crisis thing sounds an awful lot like whining doesn't it?

---

2. Just to summarize, it involves tequila, a house of questionable repute in Laredo and one very ticked off spouse. Check out the album *Exit 0*.

So, how to address it? There were, of course, the usual options:

- An affair with a young girl. Probably not an option. First of all, I possess both a mirror and a firm grip on reality. Secondly, I never dated younger women even when I could do so unembarrassed. The one woman I loved who was younger than me I married in a fiasco of biblical proportion. Next.

- Buy a Corvette. Yeah, me and whose credit rating? Besides I've never been a car guy. You know, the kind that plugs his manhood directly into the ignition? And furthermore, do they still sell Corvettes? Ah yes, once again with my finger on the pulse of the times. Even my mid-life crisis comes from a previous generation.

- Chuck it all and go on a vision quest. Maybe the most tempting option, but my Visa is maxed out and I'd have to be back for the Indian Princesses meeting on Tuesday and the standing Operations conference call on Wednesday mornings. I'm all for going crazy, but I've got responsibilities, dang it. Besides, the food on vision quests is notoriously bad.

That isn't to say that I didn't do any of the classic turning forty things, mostly of the "checking up on my immortal soul" variety. I began to read a lot of philosophy in a search for spiritual guidance. In particular, Ken Wilber makes a whole lot of sense. In a nutshell—and I'm paraphrasing/butchering this—you can't learn about, let alone talk about, something until you have actually experienced it. Meditation, spiritual enlightenment, transcendental religion can't be experienced by reading about them. You have to do them, which means meditating, reading and following some kind of practice. This isn't what I wanted to hear necessarily, but anyone who claims you can reach enlightenment any other way is probably a fraud at best.

He also talks a lot about the real truth lying beyond the reach of

standard religious practice, especially as we know it in the West. I
don't know what he means, exactly, but I'm taking it to mean that
Sunday service and covered-dish dinners (which are as close as
Methodists come to sacred rites) aren't cutting it. He also quotes a lot
of ancient philosophers, many of whom I'd actually heard of.

It's not like I'm not trying. Like so many folks of my generation, I
read the books that claim other traditions hold the eternal answers. *The
Four Agreements*, a book by Don Miguel Ruiz and based on ancient
Mexican Indian beliefs, tells us that the secret to a complete life lies in
Toltec wisdom. First of all, I quickly became aware that if the book
accurately reflects their beliefs, the Toltecs seriously lacked a sense of
humor. Furthermore, if they were so damn smart, where are all the
Toltecs? I wouldn't know one if he bit me on the butt, which is, of
course, an assumption that a Toltec would actually do such a thing, but
I don't know enough about them to make those kind of judgments.

The Art of War the ancient Chinese text by Lao Tze (not the
Wesley Snipes movie, which lacked wisdom of any kind, particularly
by the producers) was supposed to take ancient Chinese wisdom and
help us apply it to our business and personal lives to make warriors of
us all. First, I'm Canadian by birth and temperament—probably not
prime warrior material. Secondly, Lao Tze never had the Human
Resources gnomes at the office and their policies to contend with.
Tough to be a warrior when the attitude and actions it prescribes
violate the employee handbook of every corporation in America as
well as the Geneva Convention.

That doesn't mean I'm not really looking, I just find more comfort
in going back to my own, boring white-guy roots. I went back to
church a few years in advance of the 9-11 tragedies, so at least I'm not
a complete bandwagon jumper. I do take prayer and meditation a lot
more seriously than I used to. Communion took on a whole new
meaning; not so much what it means as the comfort I take in the ritual.

As un-Methodist as it may be, actual contemplation and meditation
seems to work for me—when I can find the time and the quiet. Wilber

is right; doing it does make it more relevant, at least as far as I can tell.

I know I'm getting older because while I still have major reservations about big-R Religion, small-r religion has become increasingly comforting. I can't even work up the energy to be cynical, even if the more I learn about history the less I believe the lore. Some time ago I struck a deal with God: I'll attend and take out of church what speaks to me and accept the rest as window dressing. Darned if it doesn't work.

Traditional Christianity doesn't work for me on every level, but it makes more sense to me than most of these foreign concepts. I am, after all, a forty-year-old North American. I may not know much, but I do know if spiritual fulfillment involves the Lotus position, then there's a place in hell with my name on it.

So I suppose I am on a vision quest of sorts. It's just that like most people my age, I don't want to work too hard at it. It's obvious that while I have a minor case of ants in my spiritual pants, it's not enough to send me to a mountaintop in Tibet.

At this point, it's apparent that whatever I do to indulge my forty-year itch has to be inexpensive, give me a sense of accomplishment, not be terribly disruptive to people I love, and be realistic (i.e. not too far out of my comfort zone). Having a whiff of class about it would be nice—I don't want to be the guy who turns forty and turns into a jerk. When you look at it that way, maybe I should just lie down until this feeling passes.

I need some kind of project. Something to keep my mind occupied and away from dark thoughts of boss-icide.

A hobby might be the answer. Everyone needs a hobby, right? But what should I do? What do I love more than anything else that's worth spending time and my limited resources on?

- Fishing? I can't afford a boat and my tolerance for beer isn't what it once was.
- Model trains? That is not a cheap hobby, and railroaders

are the guys the Trekkies laugh at.

♦ Collecting... What? I haven't had the time, money, or attention span to collect anything since I had the full inaugural set of 1971 Royal Bank of Canada Vancouver Canucks glossy 8x10s. This impresses no one, even if I did have Dale Tallon's rookie card, Wayne Mackie and doubles of Orland Kurtenbach.

What do I spend my money and time on now? Books mostly. Lots and lots of books. I've toyed with the idea of collecting rare books, but one trip to a serious book collector's show told me I was out of my league. When I held a leather bound edition of Sir Richard Francis Burton's *Book of the Sword* and realized that not only would my daughter never go to college if I bought it, but I may actually have to sell her to Gypsies for rent money. I wiped my chin and put it back. Yes, I am a good father, thank you very much.

Book collecting is the kind of hobby I could get into with a passion, but man, it ain't cheap. I actually made a start a while back. About five years ago, in a classy bookshop on Melrose Drive in West Hollywood I bought copies of Homer's *Iliad* and *Odyssey*. They were only $10 a piece and frankly, were the only volumes in the store I could afford. At least they were in terrific condition for being fifty years old, a fact which I'm beginning to appreciate more as I get closer to that age myself.

I asked the clerk, a Uriah Heep[3]-looking guy with very wet palms why they were so much cheaper than the other books. He looked at me with the same look of mixed disdain and pity I usually reserve for Red Sox fans and sniffed, "book club editions."

Now, you have to know that to serious book collectors, book club editions are the equivalent of buying your music from late night television. They were usually attractive, if cheaply bound, and bought

---

3. That's in the Dickens *(David Copperfield)* way vs. the '70s heavy metal band. This guy couldn't head bang his way out of a wet paper dust jacket.

by subscription. You got a bunch of them for a ridiculously low price then bought one a month until you had the whole set.

I didn't give a lot of thought to those books for a while. They looked good on the shelf, certainly better than most of the paperbacks that periodically needed to be pruned back. I'd bought a few more very old books at garage sales, mostly because they were classic titles: *The Decameron* by Boccaccio, *The Story of El Cid*, stuff like that and were old. I even bought a couple more Classics Club titles. I had just enough books to look like I was beginning a collection.

Surprisingly, most of them look brand new. In fact, my copy of *Essays and New Atlantis* by Francis Bacon cracked when I opened it and a glossy sheet of paper fell out. It was the original advertising slick, or club bulletin, as they called it. The book had never been opened, let alone read.

I scanned the club bulletin. The sales pitch went something like, "Now you can have all the Classics[4] of literature on your shelves for the low price of $2 a volume. Join the Classics Club today and receive four volumes of the greatest works of literature..." The Classics Club. The titles were certainly classics: Plato's *Republic*, *Essays of Montaigne*, and *The Collected Works of William Shakespeare*. All the great books of western civilization priced for the average guy and delivered to your door. Sign here please, payment in advance.

That phrase "have on your shelf" rang a bell with me.

It didn't say read.

It didn't say learn from.

It said, "have on your shelf." Having the books on display was the important part. They told the world that you were intelligent, classy, and erudite. In short, you were the kind of person who knew what erudite meant and could use it in a sentence. Somehow, this was important.

A phrase from the play *Auntie Mame* rattled around in my skull: "Books are awfully decorative don't you think?" Apparently a lot of

---

4. Notice the use of the capital C. Anyone can read books. These are Books, doggone it.

folks did. Who was the audience for these books?

- ◆ They were white, middle-class and middle-aged
- ◆ They obviously loved books, or at least wanted people to think they did
- ◆ They believed that what they read reflected who they are, or more to the point, what people thought they read seemed to matter an awful lot
- ◆ They obviously knew about the books, their importance to history and to our culture, but never seem to have read them

In short, they were an awful lot like me.

Why not collect the set? I wondered. They were affordable—eBay and garage sales are awash in the titles—and classy; the titles certainly give the impression that I must be a pretty smart guy. Frankly, they were the same reasons people bought them in 1942. Add a certain kitsch factor (they weren't classy enough for real collectors which had a certain appeal to my sense of the contrary) and I realized I had found something I could collect. Maybe this would help get me out of my funk, if funk it was.[5]

By the time we were ready to move to Chicago in the summer of 2001, I had ten titles of the forty available and was actively on the hunt for more. Despite dirty looks from my beloved as I made her ditch houseplants and knickknacks (paddy whacks and dog bones somehow made the trip) because they were going to be too hard to move, I carefully packed my Classics Clubs for the move to the Midwest.

As middle-aged crazy acts go, secretly spending $10 on eBay every other month won't put us in the poor house but it's transgressive enough (I never tell The Duchess when I spend the money) to let me feel like a rebel. It feels like collecting, although as a cure for the forty-blues it lacks the drama of a suicidal affair or even a good tequila bender.

---

5. I know how hard The Duchess works to put up with me when I'm like this. In the words of the immortal James Brown, "It's too funky in here."

Over time, my collection grew. I was up to fifteen…sixteen… eighteen titles. Plato, Aristotle, Balzac, Epictetus (whoever he was)— they look great on the shelf. People look suitably impressed when we show them the office. They comment on the number of tan, red and gilt volumes on the shelf. I shrug it off modestly and move to showing off the master bathroom and the magic The Duchess worked with guest towels.

Then, as it frequently does, the universe took it upon itself to kick me in the tush and put me in motion. My boss was over one night, and I showed off my collection, which he'd never seen. Now, you have to keep in mind that Pat is famous for his questioning. Staff meetings are frequently referred to behind his back as The Inquisition. Of all the grillings I've taken from him over the years, none had the psychic impact of this one.

"You've read all these?" he asked, obviously impressed.

"Read, well, ummmmmm certainly I have in other editions. These, of course are collectibles, so they're not reading copies. I mean Emerson, Plato… Hasn't everyone read them?" I fudged. Unlike at work, when he'd have nailed me to the wall like a cheap spice rack, he let me wriggle off the hook, which wasn't like him at all.

"Well, I haven't" he said it guiltily, like he should have read them.

I gained a little status jump on him at that moment. I know what he meant. He is a smart guy, who knew the books were important and he hadn't read them and somehow that mattered. Thankfully, the Duchess' towels beckoned and we left the room.

My cheeks still burn when I think about it. Why did I lie about that? Of all the stupid things. What was I thinking?

But had I read them? I could quote them like nobody's business:

"A foolish consistency is the hobgoblin of small minds."

—Emerson

"God's in his heaven, all's right with the world."

—Browning

> The Trojan Horse, the Cyclops, Penelope's weaving and
>   unweaving...   —Homer
> "His man Friday"   —Defoe

They were part of the language. Entire cultures were built on these works. Almost anyone I admired from the past was raised on this stuff. Most of the people I considered brilliant knew them intimately.

No, Pat. I hadn't read them.

Now, sometimes embarrassing admissions are just embarrassing. When you're in the depths of a full blown, hide-the-sharp-objects, where's-my-Elvis Costello-records depression, they can be galvanizing. Take action or get used to that fetal position and the taste of your own thumb, which was it going to be?

I thought about the historical figures who were the kind of people I wanted to be. Jefferson, Franklin, Sir Richard Francis Burton, Alexandre Dumas... Did these books have some kind of impact on what they were and what they'd accomplished?

Washington kept a copy of *Marcus Aurelius* by his bed. Jefferson was never without a volume of Plato. Churchill claimed Plutarch as a source of inspiration. Gandhi loved Emerson. If these books helped make those men, could a little rub off on yours truly?

They must have had an impact. I know for good or bad, the things I've read have had enormous influence on my life. *Treasure Island* and *The Three Musketeers* fanned my need for adventure and travel. Burton's biography and his travel books led me to take up fencing at the age of thirty-eight. I don't even want to think about what Bob Guccione did to my dating career.

Greeks and Romans, Persians and Americans, French and British, somehow they fused—smushed is the technical term, I believe—to form whatever it is that passes for our culture at the end of the twentieth century.

Now to be sure, there was sufficient liberal guilt in me to know that these were Dead White Males. They are no longer relevant to our lives, we've been told, and created a culture that enslaved, abused or just plain ignored huge chunks of the population. Would reading them mean I become them?

I was (and am) not prepared to give up my Canadian semi-liberal, guilt-ridden social beliefs without a fight, so if I did read them, it would be with my tongue firmly in cheek. It will involve heavy doses of careful, critical reading. Hey, if I could do it in senior high and scam an A, I can do it now. Although critical reading is not something we humans as a species have ever been very good at.[6]

Even worse, these were the big guns. Look at these titles. These are Classics with a capital C. My community college education did not contain these names. Of course, there's nothing in my academic background that says I should be training managers at Fortune 500 companies either and I've managed that trick. Maybe I can do this after all.

The fact that I've achieved some level of success in the business world—having clawed my way firmly to the middle—means one of two things:

1. formal education doesn't mean as much as I thought it did and native intelligence is enough or;
2. any day now I'll be busted, they'll realize I'm a fraud and toss me out on my ear.

From the day I began to work in the real world, I have been afraid that my lack of a university education was going to hold me back. I suffer from what could charitably be described as intellectual penis envy. I could have gone to university instead of a two-year school, but chose to make a living for fifteen years as a night club comic.

I wouldn't trade those years for anything, and it's too late to turn back now. Money, time and a loathing of pep rallies are sufficient to constrain me from actually going back to college. No, I may not have the degree, but I still have the curriculum right on my bookshelf.

---

6. For proof of this, consider the popularity and blind acceptance over the years of Mein Kampf, the Warren Commission report and The Adkins Diet.

That little voice on my shoulder whispered I might not be up to this challenge. I am a child of my generation. I grew up in the '70s. Our idea of a second language is Ebonics. In our schools, kids who can slam dunk are idolized, kids who read are wedgied and made to run the AV club and serve as Dungeon Master to the other geeks. As a society we have leapfrogged irony and gone straight to cynicism and the last autobiography I read was by The Rock.

On the other hand, why the heck not? I have a basic understanding of the history and culture these books come from. It's not like I'm going to take up Zen, with its riddles and its circular logic. Maybe I'll go there at some point, but for now this is probably enough to tackle.

There's an additional bonus that occurred to me as I stalked the local megaplex bookstore. You can pick up a brand new copy of the *Complete Works of Shakespeare* for about $15. A paperback copy of Emerson runs about $8. Anne Heche's autobiography sells for $29.95 in hard copy. Ponder the implications of *that* for a while.

First, it means you can buy great books for a lot less than you can buy newer, perhaps less great books (he says kindly).

Secondly, if that's a sign of where society places value, we're about two milliseconds away from the apocalypse. (Quick! Look over there— is that a seven-horned beast and rider on a pale horse? Never mind, it's just a squirrel) and I'm not going to feel bad putting time in on this project.

All of this is a roundabout way of saying I think I've found my project. I'm gonna get me an education. I have a new blank journal (just one of those plain lined notebooks, not one of the fancy ones you buy at Borders—I don't want to make that much of a commitment) and I'm going to record my thoughts on each book as I read it.

It's not like there's no precedent. Throughout history, writers have done this. They call them meditations. I'm not sure I'll think of anything deep enough to qualify as a meditation, but I can hope. Hell, it's not like anyone else is going to read it, right?

It may not be much, but it was a start. I doubted it would bring me eternal life or even improve the quality of the one I have now, but at least I'd be able to shake the no-college-degree monkey off my back and answer, "Yes, Pat, of course I've read them."

Not the most dramatic of mid-life crises, but it's cheaper than either a Corvette or a cocktail waitress. So, reaching for the shelf, I grabbed the first volume I came to, cracked it open and dove in....

ONE

Who the #$%^ Reads Epictetus?

The Discourses of Epictetus

"Epictetus? Who the #$%^ reads Epictetus?"

Okay, this is the first of these books I've read and there's the enlightened response from The Duchess. So much for the theory that leaving my reading conspicuously on the table while I'm sipping coffee at Borders will impress people—this may be harder than I thought.

Now, to be fair, she doesn't know I'm keeping this journal so she doesn't know this is very important research. She just thinks I'm a pretentious jerk. If I get this from the woman I love, what will complete strangers think? What if they're not impressed with my erudition? What if no one is impressed by my newfound wisdom? What if people see me reading this stuff and beat me up after school and take my lunch money?

Only I could begin my search for a mature middle age by instantly reverting to junior high.

But why did I start with *this* volume? The simple reasons are:

- I'd never heard of Epictetus, so I had no preconceptions about his relevance
- I'd know pretty early if this project were going to be an exciting intellectual journey or the Bataan Death March (note to self after page 2: pack good boots and mosquito

repellant)

- I figured it would sound really William F. Buckley-esque to drop his name: "as the Roman philosopher Epictetus once said...." and all would gawk in wonder.

Gonna have to revisit that one, judging by The Duchess' reaction.

The introductory essay gives me a pretty good picture of what I'm in for. Epictetus was a slave in Rome who rose to be a teacher of some renown, and whose writings were captured and preserved for eternity. Not a particularly original thinker, his fame seems to come from the fact that he had the good sense to write stuff down and have it survive.

Perfect, I'm looking for timeless brilliance and I get the Latin equivalent of *Chicken Soup for the Soul*.

Let's see what he has to say for himself....

The first few pages are full of sage advice, nothing my father didn't tell me, but on page ten I'm slapped in the face by the following:

"... Thus acted also a wrestler, who was in danger of death unless his private parts were amputated. His brother, who was a philosopher, came to him and said, "Well Brother, what do you propose to do? Shall we cut off this part, and return again to the field?" He refused, and courageously died.

'When someone asked whether he acted thus as a wrestler, or as a Philosopher, I answers as a man, but as a man who had been proclaimed champion at the Olympic games; who had been used to such places and not merely rubbed down in the School of Berto.[7] Another would have his very head cut off if he could have lived without it. This is what regard for character, so powerful with those who are accustomed of their own accord to consider it in their deliberations..."

---

7. This means he was a real wrestler and not just some gym rat. Apparently hanging out at Gold's gym in the hopes someone will be impressed is not a new phenomenon.

Hold on there Babba Looey.

My first reaction was, "What the heck did this guy have?"

My second reaction was, I probably won't ever be a really great philosophic mind unless I can stop giggling when I see the words "private parts were amputated" in a book.

Now, this is the kind of discussion I'd expect to hear in a bar, rather than in a classic of Latin thought. After all, in a way, this is a slightly more extreme version of the time-honored "Should he pitch with a torn rotator cuff?" argument. And let's face it, as something to make men cry it has *Brian's Song* beat six ways to Sunday. But all that aside, what is he really talking about there?

On the surface, the point of the story is this: The wrestler decided that he wasn't about to cut his, ummmm, manhood off, and died as a result, but at least he was a man about it. Now, I'm not sure I'd make that decision personally. Let's analyze the case of whether I would amputate my private parts or not:

Pro	Con
◆ It's my life we're talking about here!	◆ Over the years it has taken a leading role in my decision making
◆ It was never much to write home about	◆ Even if I lost that thirty pounds, a Speedo swimsuit is now out of the question
◆ Except for every other Saturday night, no one else will miss it much either	

In short, I'd operate and old Epictetus can go pound sand.

According to the essay up front, our boy Epictetus was a Stoic. As my eight-year-old would say, No DUH! Apparently Stoic is the old Greek word for hardass.

But the story is not about whether it is more manly to die than to cut off your Johnson. This was a world-class wrestler. He wasn't just any old hanger-on in the gym. He'd been an Olympic champion. He made a choice and lived (or in this case died) by that choice.

In other words: Decide on what's important to you, stick to it, and don't whine.

Well, what do you know? My Old Man isn't a hard case, he's a Stoic. So were his parents. I'm guessing so were theirs. What happened to me and my generation?

As I write this, I'm watching MSNBC out of the corner of my eye and they're reporting on a group of people launching a class action lawsuit against Osama Bin Laden for creating undue mental stress. Apparently not a Stoic in that bunch anywhere.

As I get older, I realize I'm becoming more and more Stoic in my outlook. In fact, I often wonder how old I have to be before I can officially be a curmudgeon.[8] My patience with whiners is becoming less and less, and the whiner I'm most tired of is me.

My job stinks, the people I work for have their heads lodged somewhere dark and funky, I'm getting fat... Well, Bucko, change jobs or deal with it, help them get smarter or shut up, do some sit ups or quit complaining. When you think about it my options are fairly well defined.

In my heart I believe that the laws ought to have a "Stuff Happens" clause. "Stuff" is, of course, a personal term. You are free to put in whatever euphemism works for you. Before you sue somebody you should have to ask yourself, is this the result of action someone took, or is it just plain old bad luck—in other words, stuff? If they did something truly malicious or illegal, have at them and I hope they pay through the nose. If they didn't, realize that life is often unfair and get back to work. I'm sorry you hit that tree with your car but the U.S. Forest Service is probably not responsible for letting it grow there. Case dismissed, let's move on.

Okay, smart guy, so you've decided to just stop whining and take

---

8. At some point you are old enough to be a curmudgeon. Before that you're simply a raving jerk. It's a variation of the eternal question; "How much money do you have to have before you're eccentric?" Above a certain income level you're eccentric. Beneath it, you're just a loon. Life is full of such quandaries.

whatever comes. Is it that simple? Does it mean you just take whatever comes your way and live with it? What does that mean for my activist liberal politics? Do we accept bad government or morally wrong laws? At what point does Stoicism become helplessness, which becomes apathy, which becomes inertia, which becomes laziness.

I doubt that's what it means. Epictetus was born a slave, but he didn't end up one. Obviously at some point he decided to take action and not accept the status quo. Does he mean if you are going to pick a hill to die on, accept the consequences of that choice? If it means jail, or martyrdom, or just having the neighbors ticked off at you, that's the price you pay.

Gonna have to work on this one a bit.

My goodness. That's quite a tangent I've wandered off on and I'm only on page 10.

So, back to Epictetus and what he has to say for himself... For the next hundred pages or so, there are a lot of fancy ways of saying "Don't complain," "Deal with it," and "Get over yourself."

"For the present, endure to remain at this post where [God] has placed you. The time of your abode here is short and easy for men like you; for what tyrant, what thief, or what court can be formidable to those who count as nothing the body and its possessions."

"...see the origin of Tragedy, when trifling accidents befall foolish men. 'Ah, when shall I see Athens and the citadel again?' Foolish man, are you not contented with what you see every day? Can you see anything better than the sun, the moon, the stars, the whole earth, the sea? But, if besides, you comprehend him who administers the whole, and carry him about within yourself, do you still long after certain stones and fine rock?"

In other words, you don't need an X-box for Christmas, so shut up. Generally speaking, this is not soul-inspiring stuff, although it makes for cool quotes at the start of employee memos.

I love starting memos with quotes, it makes things seem more authoritative. For example: "You can be unconquerable, if you enter into no combat in which it is not in your own power to conquer. When, therefore, you see anyone eminent in honors or power, or in high esteem on any other account, take heed not to be bewildered by appearances and pronounce him happy; for if the essence of good consists in things within our own power, there will be no room for envy or jealousy."

That sounds so much better than "We regret to inform you your request for promotion has been denied at this time."

At first, I thought about how so many other people have said the same thing over the years. It's usually followed by something about God's will and mysterious ways. The interesting fact here for me is that Epictetus was not a Christian. The things he talks about—and let's not forget he borrowed from Greeks, Persians, and other people who came before him—predate Christianity, Calvinism or even my Aunt Heather.

These sometimes boring, often trite, and ultimately all too true sentiments have been around a lot longer than almost any idea. Like any story that's been around that long, it must have a core of truth.[9]

That truth is why I'm doing this I think. Why else am I wading through all these old books and risking the mockery of The Duchess—to discover things I've been told all my life.

I think I'm looking at what has been true since people started scribbling on cave walls. If it was true for Epictetus—and Benjamin Franklin and Balzac and the guy in the park feeding pigeons and swearing to himself—odds are pretty good it's probably true for me. It feels true, at least. The truth be told, and cynicism aside, that feels strangely comforting.

Just as I'm feeling all warm and fuzzy, though, that darn Stoic smooshes a reality pie in my face. In a discussion on my philosophy matters, he informs me:

---

9. I'm not 100 percent sure about this. There is, after all, that story about Richard Gere and the gerbil that just won't go away.

"There must be some rule. And why do we not seek and discover it, and when we have discovered, ever after make use of it, without fail, so as not even to move a finger without it? For this, I conceive, is what, when found, will cure those of their madness who make use of no other measure but their own perverted way of thinking. Afterwards, beginning from certain known and determinate points, we may make use of general principles, properly applied to particulars."

After reading that, I looked over my shoulder, half expecting to see Epictetus looking over my shoulder. I felt so busted.

Long after I put Epictetus back on the shelf this has stuck with me. Whether you believe he has the right definition of those "known and determinate points" or not, he makes a case that's hard to shake: Once you find those rules, you can no longer ignore them. They should be a conscious part of every decision and action you take.

That's not a casual thought.

So which selection to include? This one struck me as important only because it talks about improving for the sake of improving. Hey, it's as good a reason as any....

OF PROGRESS OR IMPROVEMENT
— Epictetus

He who is making progress, having learned from philosophers that desire means the desire of good things, and aversion means aversion from bad things; having learned too that happiness and tranquillity are not attainable by man otherwise than by not failing to obtain what he desires, and not falling into that which he would avoid; such a man takes from himself desire altogether and defers it, but he employs his aversion only on things which are dependent on his will.

For if he attempts to avoid anything independent of his will, he knows that sometimes he will fall in with something which he wishes to avoid, and he will be unhappy. Now if virtue promises good fortune and tranquility and happiness, certainly also the progress toward virtue is progress toward each of these things. For it is always true that to whatever point the perfecting of anything leads us, progress is an approach toward this point.[10]

How then do we admit that virtue is such as I have said, and yet seek progress in other things and make a display of it? What is the product of virtue? Tranquility. Who then makes improvement? It is he who has read many books of Chrysippus? But does virtue consist in having understood Chrysippus?

If this is so, progress is clearly nothing else than knowing a great deal of Chrysippus. But now we admit that virtue produces one thing, and we declare that approaching near to it is another thing, namely, progress or improvement. "Such a person," says one, "is already able to read Chrysippus by himself." Indeed, sir, you are making great progress. What kind of progress? But why do you mock the man? Why do you draw him away from the perception of his own misfortunes?

Will you not show him the effect of virtue that he may learn where to look for improvement? Seek it there, wretch, where your work lies. And where is your work? In desire and in aversion, that you may not be disappointed in your desire, and that you may not fall into that which you would avoid; in your pursuit and avoiding, that you commit no error; in assent and suspension of assent, that you be not deceived.

The first things, and the most necessary, are those which I have named. But if with trembling and lamentation you seek not to fall into that which you avoid, tell me how you are improving.

Do you then show me your improvement in these things? If I were talking to an athlete, I should say, "Show me your shoulders"; and then he might say, "Here are my halteres." You and your halteres look to that.

---

10. Okay, breathe. If you haven't read much philosophy before, I hate to break it to you but that was fairly elementary stuff. Look at it this way, by warming up with Epictetus you won't pull a hamstring when you get to Plato.

I should reply, "I wish to see the effect of the halteres." So, when you say: "Take the treatise on the active powers, and see how I have studied it."

I reply, "Slave, I am not inquiring about this, but how you exercise pursuit and avoidance, desire and aversion, how your design and purpose and prepare yourself, whether conformably to nature or not. If conformably, give me evidence of it, and I will say that you are making progress: but if not conformably, be gone, and not only expound your books, but write such books yourself; and what will you gain by it?

"Do you not know that the whole book costs only five denarii? Does then the expounder seem to be worth more than five denarii? Never, then, look for the matter itself in one place, and progress toward it in another."

Where then is progress? If any of you, withdrawing himself from externals, turns to his own will to exercise it and to improve it by labour, so as to make it conformable to nature, elevated, free, unrestrained,unimpeded, faithful, modest; and if he has learned that he who desires or avoids the things which are not in his power can neither be faithful nor free, but of necessity he must change with them and be tossed about with them as in a tempest, and of necessity must subject himself to others who have the power to procure or prevent what he desires or would avoid; finally, when he rises in the morning, if he observes and keeps these rules, bathes as a man of fidelity, eats as a modest man; in like manner, if in every matter that occurs he works out his chief principles as the runner does with reference to running, and the trainer of the voice with reference to the voice—this is the man who truly makes progress, and this is the man who has not traveled in vain.

But if he has strained his efforts to the practice of reading books, and labours only at this, and has traveled for this, I tell him to return home immediately, and not to neglect his affairs there; for this for which he has traveled is nothing.

But the other thing is something, to study how a man can rid his life of lamentation and groaning, and saying, "Woe to me," and "wretched that I am," and to rid it also of misfortune and disappointment and to learn what death is, and exile, and prison, and poison, that he may be able to say when he is in fetters, "Dear Crito, if it is the will of the gods that it be so, let it be so"; and not to say, "Wretched am I, an old man; have I kept my gray hairs for this?" Who is it that speaks thus?

Do you think that I shall name some man of no repute and of low condition?

Does not Priam say this? Does not Oedipus say this? Nay, all kings say it! For what else is tragedy than the perturbations of men who value externals exhibited in this kind of poetry?

But if a man must learn by fiction that no external things which are independent of the will concern us, for this part I should like this fiction, by the aid of which I should live happily and undisturbed. But you must consider for yourselves what you wish.

What then does Chrysippus teach us? The reply is, "to know that these things are not false, from which happiness comes and tranquility arises. Take my books, and you will learn how true and conformable to nature are the things which make me free from perturbations."

O great good fortune! O the great benefactor who points out the way! To Triptolemus all men have erected temples and altars, because he gave us food by cultivation; but to him who discovered truth and brought it to light and communicated it to all, not the truth which shows us how to live, but how to live well, who of you for this reason has built an altar, or a temple, or has dedicated a statue, or who worships God for this?

Because the gods have given the vine, or wheat, we sacrifice to them; but because they have produced in the human mind that fruit by which they designed to show us the truth which relates to happiness, shall we not thank God for this?

TWO

The Jiffy Lube Theory of Marriage

Poems of Robert Browning

> Beautiful Evelyn Hope is dead!
>   Sit and watch by her side an hour.
> That is her book shelf, this her bed;
>   She plucked that piece of geranium-flower,
> Beginning to die too, in the glass;
>   Little has yet been changed, I think:
> The shutters are shut, no light may pass
>   Save two long rays thro' the hinges chink...
>   —Robert Browning, "Evelyn Hope," 1855

Well, this guy's a fun date.

Poetry. This is going to be grim. I was never a poetry guy. Even when in the depths of my tortured young wannabe writer pretensions, poetry didn't figure into the equation.

When was the last time I voluntarily read poetry? I'm a child of the '70s post-"Howl,"—the Allan Ginsberg poem from the late '50s that's the epitome of beatnik tom tom-beating, finger-snapping poetry—which as near as I can work out was the last poem that really mattered to the world at large. Certainly the last one anyone in North America can name.

25

The reason, and darn it I'll say it, is that the people who used to write poetry have all become song writers. Sensitive youths with pasty skin and black T-shirts who want to gnash their teeth or howl at the moon now do it with a guitar. The reasons are pretty simple:

- That's where the money is
- That's the only way the kind of guys who write poetry can get laid, and even then only by the kind of women who like poetry.[11]

There's rap, of course. Poetry of the streets, they say, and that may be true, I just can't get into it. I want to. When rap became the driving force in pop, and I was still reading *Rolling Stone* in an attempt to be musically literate, I tried, but all that scratching was too annoying for my Canadian ears.

I want to respect rap, I really do. First of all, anything people put that much time and effort into should not be dismissed out of hand. I have to admit, though, I have a visceral gut-tightening reaction to the phrase "yo-yo-yo." I have given this a lot of thought because the initial reaction to suburban middle-aged white people who don't like rap is that it's a racial issue. I hope and pray that it's not. I've looked at it, analyzed it and pulled out my official Ronco "Liberal Self-Flogomatic" and worn it to a nub and the fact is, it's just not my thing.

It's the anger, mostly; the celebration of the ugly and the embracing of the worst in human nature. Now, why it's any worse than the blues or country music I've listened to all my life I'm not sure—it just is. Also, I thought we'd gotten past the need to play records backwards after we discovered Paul was not really dead. Let's be honest, "Keeping it real" is the new-millennium phrase for "Tell it like it is," a phrase that protest bands used in the '60s, and usually meant the refusal to discuss the issue calmly, bad poetry and worse hair.

No, I suspect that it's cultural more than racial and that's an entirely

---

11. Pull out your encyclopedias and look up Morrison, Jim for the first example of the tortured teenage poet-geek elevated to Rock Star status resulting in female adoration far above the way he actually filled out those leather pants. See also, Dylan, Bob and Ian, Janis.

different issue. There is a difference between race and culture. I am a
forty-year-old, hockey-watching, Canadian, alleged Methodist, father of
a kid with an unnatural fondness for Chicago blues, John Hiatt and
Mendelssohn. Rap music isn't for me, it's *about* me, and I reserve the
right not to like it.[12]

The fact that I am white has never stopped me from loving and
adopting Black culture or language when it appealed to me. Blues, soul,
reggae have always spoken to me in very strong ways. What's true is
true, and any art can cross boundaries, although the traffic definitely
flows easier one way.

People say that Elvis was a musical pioneer for bringing black
music to a white audience. True enough, but you wanna know a real
brave soul? Charlie Pride. Try being a black country and western singer
in the '60s. This was the days before video, and I'm willing to bet more
than one club owner got a rude shock when Charlie showed up to play.
"Sorry 'bout firehosing you at the door, Charlie. No hard feelings,
right?" Long as it wasn't a white angel he was kissing good morning,
Charlie was alright with them.

Nope, rap doesn't cut it for me, and I refuse to feel bad about that.

Okay, I just thought of a poet I can actually name. There's Maya
Angelou, and I do feel bad about not liking her work. Truth is, her stuff
always has that whiff of "take it it's good for you" about it. She's an
African-American woman and that always seems to be the most
important thing. I'm supposed to respect whatever comes after that
whether it works for me or not. I'm sorry, but I don't have to like
something or think it's aesthetically pleasing, even if I agree with its
sentiments. I gave up agenda art back in the eighties.

Here I sit, Browning in hand, gearing up to read poetry with about
as much eagerness as Pat Buchanan at a Cinco de Mayo party. Poetry

---

12. I should confess that Public Enemy did furnish me with one of the great comeback lines of all
time. "Motherf@#$ you and John Wayne" is one hell of a show-stopper. I used it once to get a sales
manager off my back after another missed deadline. Even without citing the source, he knew I
meant it, if not what the heck I meant. Check out Public Enemy's, "Fight the Power." You heard it
at the end of *Do the Right Thing,* if you weren't too busy cowering under your seat.

will forever be associated with English class, suicidal teenage girls
(Sylvia Plath as role model…good idea or romantic silliness, discuss
amongst yourselves) or fans of the dirty limerick. (Note to self: really
have to visit Nantucket some day.)

It occurs to the Philistine side of me that one reason books of poetry
don't sell is they don't seem like very good bargains. They don't use up
the whole page, there's a lot of white space and, compared to a good
Tom Clancy paperback you certainly don't get much for your money.
Yup, it's artistic criticism like that that got me where I am today, folks.

I'll admit, Browning snuck up on me. At first, I enjoyed what I read
but shrugged it off. It was a lot of work, and make no mistake, poetry is
hard work. Unfamiliar words (what in the name of Elizabeth Barret is a
"wattled cote?" [13]) and strained rhymes[14] make for slow going. To make
it worse, I was never sure of the meter. My untrained ears were never
sure where I should be putting the emphasis.

Here's a trick, and you'll have to go with me on this one. It all
turned around when I read it out loud. This is enough of a trick, I grant
you. Mrs. Armstrong pretty much whacked oral reading out of me in
third grade. But once I started to read the poems out loud, and with a
British accent no less, the words fell into place more logically. I began
to appreciate them.

I didn't appreciate my eight-year-old rolling her eyes when she
caught me at it. Her Serene Highness gave me her most superior look
and sneered, "Mrs. Fougerousse says grown-ups don't have to read out
loud—we do silent reading in third grade now." Yeah, well Mrs.
Fougerousse isn't trying to reconcile "determined" and "sun-burned."

I didn't think it was sticking with me, until the other day in a sales
meeting of all places. I had missed yet another deadline, and the sales
weasel—I'm sorry, account executive—was all over me about it.

---

13. I am at your service. It turns out a wattled cote is a mud-covered pigeon coop. I'm guessing that
the ability to make something like that sound romantic is a big factor in Browning's appeal.
14. Of course, nothing like in country music. Bocephus (Hank Williams Jr. to the uninitiated) can
rhyme "drink" and "Hank" like nobody's business. Don't even get me started on Dylan.

I leaned back in my chair, full of confidence I didn't feel, and smiled. What I meant to say was "Steps we took in the first quarter should show results by summer."

What came out was "June reared the bunch of flowers you carry from seeds of April's sowing."

It sprang out of my mouth unbidden. Now the last thing you want to do to anyone that far behind quota is spring something like that on him. It wasn't received in the spirit intended, and caught me as off guard as it did the sales weasel. Still, I love that phrase, and it stuck with me. If only Browning had a pithy phrase for "get off your ass and cold call," I'd have been in really good shape.

That's, I think, what I took away from reading Browning. The phrase, like a burr on a sock, had latched on and hitched a ride on my brain. The phrase, the exact right words to paint a picture, a metaphor so perfect that nothing else will do. You have to dig through a ton of poetry to find one but when you do, it's a keeper. Also, chicks dig it.

And they do. Boy, do they ever.

I defy any even partially heterosexual woman to read the following passage without shooting daggers at her husband or boyfriend...

> She should never have looked at me
> If she meant I should not love her!
> There are plenty...men you call such,
> I suppose... she may discover
> All her soul to, if she pleases
> And yet leave much as she found them:
> But, I'm not so and she knew it
> When she fixed me glancing round them
> —Robert Browning, "Cristina," 1850

Browning was a Romantic with a capitol R. In his day, men would use his poetry to seduce women. Unmarried women would read it to rationalize why they couldn't find a man up to their standards. And Browning used it, particularly after Elizabeth died, to be a very sought after dinner guest (ten bucks says it wasn't husbands making the invitations).

We have something in common, he and I. We both married women older than ourselves, and after youths of some uhhhh adventure, settled in to monogamy with nary a whimper and loved our wives like crazy. (I say loved, because Elizabeth died. The Duchess is still very much with me.) Like Browning, I have been accused of being a romantic. Unlike Browning, it's largely undeserved.

Yes, I exhibit the signs of hopeless romanticism—a phrase I detest. In my younger days I insisted on being called a hope*ful* romantic. Much more positive and guaranteed to melt even the most reluctant ice princess. God bless women's gullible little hearts.

> I call The Duchess "my bride" even after more than ten years together.
>
> I bring home flowers unexpectedly.
>
> I make a point of taking her on dates, even if it's just for cocktails and chicken wings, it's cocktails and chicken wings without Her Serene Highness demanding our nonstop adoration.
>
> I feel bad if a day goes by without my actually uttering the phrase, "I love you."

Those of you men who want to kick my butt at this point, line forms to the left. Before you do, though, you should look at the other line forming to the right. Your wives and girlfriends are ready to nominate me for a Nobel prize.

I don't claim to be special, but after a spectacularly failed first marriage, I am determined to do better this time around, and so I operate under what I call the "Jiffy Lube Theory of Marriage."[15] It goes like this:

> Every man in America knows you should change the oil on your car every 3,000 miles. They also know that they can go way longer without

---

15. Sad but true, you can get men to listen to almost anything if it has an analogy to cars or sports. You want to know why we don't leave the seat down? Because it isn't in the owner's manual and Vince Lombardi never had anything to say about the topic.

causing actual damage, but if they get into the habit
1. they won't get lazy about it and let it go too long, causing real damage;
2. they'll spot problems before they leave you stranded and alone somewhere;
3. the car will last longer, saving time and money down the road.

By doing some very simple things with their wives, they can solve these problems:
1. they won't get lazy about it and let it go too long, causing real damage;
2. they'll spot problems before they leave you stranded and alone somewhere;
3. the marriage will last longer, saving time and money down the road.

Now, here's where it gets tricky, so you may want to take notes. While these have all the earmarks of very romantic behaviors, they are actually grounded in more mundane, if not outright cynical, truths.

First off, it helps if you realize that love is not a noun, it's a verb. It's not something you're in, or something you have, it's something that you do. If you love something, you invest time and effort in it. Sometimes, it's rotating your tires, sometimes it's bringing home a $5 bouquet from Safeway.

The secret is to do it regularly. Unusual behavior arouses suspicion. This is why men who only buy flowers when they've screwed up are so easily busted. Men who do it all the time are cut slack for the hundred little screwups we commit on a daily basis. Preventative maintenance gentlemen. Trust me on this.

It's not really that difficult once you get into the habit. If you can't bring yourself to say, "I love you" on a regular basis, try this one. We know women are more aroused by scent than men. Most women love to dress their man. They would love to pick out your clothes and cologne. How many men wear the clothes their ladies buy for them? What would be the reaction if when they ask, "You're not wearing that are you?" your response was to ask for a suggestion instead of snorting and saying, "Yeah, I only wore it one day."

I think Shakespeare put it best when he said, "DUH!"

It doesn't hurt if you mean what you say, either. Amazing thing about The Duchess, every time I say the scheduled "I love you" the little voice inside my head says, "Damned if I don't."

Mushiness aside, and lord knows there's enough of it in Browning, it's more enjoyable than I thought. I like the act of reading aloud, which is something I haven't done in ages. I even shared a poem or two with The Duchess, which had the desired amorous effect.[16]

I don't know if I can make a habit of poetry, but it wasn't as onerous a task as I thought it was going to be, and the experiment did result in one ticked off sales person and one moderately satisfied wife (and it wasn't even Saturday!), and that's not a bad day's work.

IN THREE DAYS
— Robert Browning, 1855

1
So, I shall see her in three days
And just one night, but nights are short,
Then two long hours, and that is morn.
See how I come, unchanged, unworn!
Feel, where my life broke off from thine,
How fresh the splinters keep and fine,—
Only a touch and we combine!
2
Too long, this time of year, the days!
But nights, at least the nights are short.

---

16. Again, a shameful admission. Almost anything that sounds like poetry, if read in a soft and gushing manner, will have the desired amorous effect. One of the most amazing nights of my life was kicked off by a reading of Song of Solomon straight out of the King James Bible. Her breasts were nothing like two does come to drink, but hey, it worked.

As night shows where ger one moon is,
A hand's-breadth of pure light and bliss,
So life's night gives my lady birth
And my eyes hold her! What is worth
The rest of heaven, the rest of earth?

3
O loaded curls, release your store
Of warmth and scent, as once before
The tingling hair did, lights and darks
Outbreaking into fairy sparks,
When under curl and curl I pried
After the warmth and scent inside,
Thro' lights and darks how manifold—
The dark inspired, the light controlled
As early Art embrowns the gold.

4
What great fear, should one say, "Three days
That change the world might change as well
Your fortune; and if joy delays,
Be happy that no worse befell!"
What small fear, if another says,
"Three days and one short night beside
May throw no shadow on your ways;
But years must teem with change untried,
With chance not easily defied,
With an end somewhere undescried."
No fear!—or if a fear be born
This minute, it dies out in scorn.
Fear? I shall see her in three days
And one night, now the nights are short,
Then just two hours, and that is morn.

THREE

F. Bacon, Renaissance Management Consultant

Essays of Francis Bacon

Okay, I confess that I dread reading some of these books because they'll be dull. I can handle dull; I am, after all, a public high school graduate. There are others I dread for an entirely different reason—the author is so much smarter than I am that is intimidating as hell.

Bacon is one of these guys I've always admired, not that I've read his work, but his reputation more than precedes him. He was literally a Renaissance man. Let's look for a moment at his resume:

- politician
- poet
- essayist
- scientist
- convicted felon

Not only did he do all of these things, he was *really good* at them (except for the felony part, which was petty ante and he did time for it). He was not just a politician; he was a great writer and was one of the few Englishmen respected in Europe.

That's not enough for you? He died in the name of science. Okay, it would have been more romantic had he died of radiation poisoning like Madame Curie. What happened was, he actually caught pneumonia and died stuffing a chicken full of snow to see what would happen. That's so Bacon, finding out why he crossed the road wasn't enough, he had to find out what would happen if he crossed the road with a backside full of snow. Apparently this was a pressing question in the Middle Ages. Most philosophers wanted to be Aristotle, he wanted to be Clarence Birdseye.[17]

Oh yeah, and he did time for bribery. Pretty much a full plate.

So I plunged in and got a pretty rude shock; he may have been all those things, but exciting he was not. It's a tough read; pack a lunch. Not only is he a firm believer in the value of the multi-syllable word, but he tends to make his really strong points in Latin, which means lots of footnotes and wondering what he's really trying to say.

You'll find that a lot in these books by the way. Somehow saying it in Latin made it more authoritative, which is true if authority is defined as saying it in the most roundabout way possible. (Actually since anyone who could read back then read Latin, it was actually a kind of shorthand. They never took the twenty-first century into account.) It also assumes that a dead Roman guy is more believable than the person writing the essay.

Let me give you an example of what I'm talking about. In his essay "Of Great Place," which is his treatise that basically says, Be careful what you ask for because once you achieve great things, it's all down hill from there. (I paraphrase, but since Bacon achieved dizzying heights then took one of the more spectacular career tumbles, the man is qualified—unlike Alec Baldwin who just needs to shut the hell up.) In translation it says, It is a sad fate for a man to die too well known to others, and to himself unknown, which is a pretty pithy statement and worth reading. However, in Latin it reads *Illi mors gravis incubat, qui*

---

17. Clarence Birdseye (yes, as in Birds Eye frozen foods) continued the long respected white guy tradition of taking things native people had been doing for centuries and making a buck out of it. While living in Labrador in the early 1900s, he noticed that local natives froze food quickly, preserving its taste (more or less). He invented a machine that could do just that and the rest is history. Yes, unfortunately for the indigenous Labradorians, they invented the TV dinner, not the patent office.

notus nimi omnibus, ignotus moritur sibi, which, if you're like me, pretty much means it's cocktail hour.

Since no one our age has actually studied Latin, this makes reading pretty much like crossing a parking lot—short bursts of progress followed by a big old speed bump. Do yourself a favor, if you are going to read Bacon, or anyone from that time period, find a translation that puts the English translation in the text and Latin in the footnote.

This reading tip brought to you by the Coalition to Not Make Yourself Crazy, and the Ad Council.

Bacon knew his Greeks and Latins, but he also knew anyone who had written pretty much anything at the time. He knew of, and roundly endorsed, Machiavelli's writing. The Sufis of the Middle East say his writing was based on Arab texts from Spain and claim Bacon as one of their own. Of course, the Sufis claim anyone who wasn't a complete idiot as one of their own,[18] but that's another discussion for another day. The point is, he was a player.

And yet...

He couldn't walk the talk. He wrote convincingly and knowledgeably about honor, and being all you can be, and shouldering responsibility, which is pretty gutsy for someone doing time in the slam for taking bribes. Rather than turn me off, I confess, it made me want to read him even more and slog through a hundred Latin quotes if I had to.

Let's face it, in these times of Clinton and Condit, Jesse Jackson, and Enron—and Lord knows who all—someone whose hubris brought them to such a crashing halt probably has something legitimate to say. I took it in the spirit of anyone who goes to a white-collar prison and does what they all do: become a management consultant.

This idea of Bacon as the first Western European consultant (actually Machiavelli would have been the true first, but he was so evil in a blatant Dick Morris kind of way I've disqualified him) occurred to me when I came across this in his essay "Of Innovation":

---

18. In *The Sufis* by Idries Shah, you'll find the whole list of who they're claiming for their own.

"It were good, therefore, that men in their innovations would follow the example of time itself, which indeed innovateth greatly, but quietly, and by degrees scarce to be perceived; for otherwise, whatsoever is new is unlooked for and ever it mends some and pairs others; and he that is holpen, takes it for a fortune, and thanks the time; and he that is hurt, for a wrong and imputeth it to the author."

So, long before change management consultants got paid big bucks, anyone's cheese went anywhere, or people like me got paid to impart stale clichés to middle management—well anyone other than the village priest anyway—the wisdom was there for anyone to find: .

- People will accept only gradual (if not glacial) change
- If it helps them, they'll think it's a good idea
- If it's a pain in the butt, they'll take it out on the messenger
- What else do you need to know?

Yup, people don't like change, never have, never will. It took seventeen kazillion copies of "Who Moved My Cheese" later to learn that. Sometimes it's even worse than that. "I know precisely where my cheese is, I'm just lactose intolerant." They don't even care where it's gone, because at the end of the day it's cheese, for Pete's sake.

This is not universally true, of course. I like change; I crave it. Call it wanderlust, or dissatisfaction with mediocrity or corporate ADD, but I need the rush of change. First one on the bus and ready to ride, that's me. Not, by the way, an attitude guaranteed to make you the most popular kid in school.

Heck that's why I am living in the western suburbs of Chicago, because I'd been in one place ten years and by golly it was movin' on time. Never mind that The Duchess didn't want to go and Her Serene Highness never thought of leaving Nana or California.

One thing I have learned in the existential zigzag from Mission to Vancouver, to Toronto, to Los Angeles to Chicago: Not everyone adjusts to change at the same speed as I do. Heck, I've had cars that don't adjust at the speed I do, but then that's just me.

Something eerie happened while I was reading this book, and if anything in this journal forms a pattern, it's shaping up to be this: At least once while reading each of these books, something I read corresponded exactly to something going on in my life that's causing stress. In this case, it involves The Duchess, Her Serene Highness and just about every married man in the world.

There reach points in every person's life when you question the choices you've made. Are the people you love, no matter how much you love them, holding you back? Could you be so much more than what you are if you weren't shackled down with the responsibility of others?

This wasn't the first time I'd asked this question in my life. Well, actually the first Mrs. Turmel asked the question first, but I got around to asking it eventually. I certainly had good reason to ask it. My stand-up career pretty much ended when my daughter was born.

Just before the arrival of HSH I had done my first national American television slot. *Evening at the Improv*, while plankton level show business, was an important credit to a road comic like me. The problem was that now I was married with a newborn daughter. The things I needed to do to build on my career—hang out at the LA comedy clubs till all hours scrounging stage time, taking gigs for little money but great exposure—those things were no longer options. So, what momentum I had withered away until at last, it was day-job city.

I've loved my corporate career. Few have been as lucky in their lives as I have to give up something they love and find something else they love nearly as much. But as I stare at the ceiling tiles in the wee small hours I sometimes ask, "What could I be if I were alone?" They're not the moments I'm proud of, but Lord knows they come, bidden or not.

I was going through one of these bouts of examination/self pity when I came across this line in "Of Marriage and Single Life":

"He that hath wife and children hath given hostages to fortune; for they are impediments to great enterprises, either of virtue or mischief."

Well, ain't that, to quote the great philosopher Dean Martin, a kick in the head?

Why should that be? Why is it so hard to achieve great things when you have a wife and kids? Look at the great artists, scientists, and others. Most of them either did their best work before they were married or while they basically ignored and/or abused their loved ones by being completely self-absorbed.

The reason for this I believe (assuming you can exclude details like talent and actual commitment) is, as Bacon says, you've given up hostages. Everything you do from now on has to be balanced against the needs of other people, and the things that you have to do to be successful at anything, whether it's in business, the arts or anything else are inherently selfish.

Think about the networking, the long hours, the inattention to the needs of wives and children that go into the success story of almost anyone you can think of. Einstein, Picasso, Bing Crosby—you get the picture.

Does that mean it's impossible to be a good family man and a success? Obviously not, but it is exponentially harder. I suspect that's why so few women reach the top in those fields—it's not lack of ability, it's the choices they make (or, to be fair, often have made for them). I've made my choices in life, and now I'm reaping the rewards. No sense moping.

The amazing thing is that despite wondering what might have been—and I do a lot less of that as time goes by and become more Stoic in my outlook—I am satisfied with what I've got and become. On reading Bacon's line again, I think I know why.

That "either of virtue or mischief" is the key, methinks. True, I will not be running off to join the Peace Corps or become a monk or do any of the other noble things I fantasize about. There are ballet lessons to pay for and cable bills to meet after all. At the same time I am far less likely to do something terminally stupid.

Yeah, I may never win an Oscar, or a Nobel Prize or even Employee of the Month, but I'm also not likely to face incarceration, rehab or something even penicillin won't cure.

Am I okay with that? Mostly. The thing to watch out for is that acceptance of limitations does not become complacence. That settling for the best you can do is not the same thing as settling for mediocrity.

Boy, nothing comes easily does it?

This essay talks about studying and learning. If you're reading this book, it's probably preaching to the choir, but then it's tough slogging and if it's gonna be this much work you may as well agree with its conclusions....

OF STUDIES
— Francis Bacon, 1625

Studies serve for delight, for ornament, and for ability. Their chief use for delight, is in privateness and retiring; for ornament, is in discourse; and for ability, is in the judgment, and disposition of business. For expert men can execute, and perhaps judge of particulars, one by one; but the general counsels, and the plots and marshalling of affairs, come best, from those that are learned. To spend too much time in studies is sloth; to use them too much for ornament, is affectation; to make judgment wholly by their rules, is the humor of a scholar. They perfect nature, and are perfected by experience: for natural abilities are like natural plants, that need proyning, by study; and studies themselves, do give forth directions too much at large, except they be bounded in by experience. Crafty men contemn studies, simple men admire them, and wise men use them; for they teach not their own use; but that is a wisdom without them, and above them, won by observation. Read not to contradict and confute; nor to believe and take for granted; nor to find talk and discourse; but to weigh and consider. Some books are to be tasted, others to be swallowed, and some few to be chewed and digested; that is, some books are to be read only in parts; others to be read, but not curiously; and some few to be read wholly, and with diligence and attention. Some books also may be read by deputy, and extracts made of them by others; but that would be only in the less important arguments, and the meaner sort of books, else distilled books are like common distilled waters, flashy things. Reading maketh a full man; conference a ready man; and writing an exact man. And therefore, if a man write little, he had need have a great memory; if he confer little, he had need have a present wit: and if he read little, he had need have much cunning, to seem to know, that he doth not. Histories make men wise; poets witty; the mathematics subtile; natural philosophy deep; moral grave; logic and rhetoric able to contend. *Abeunt studia in mores.* Nay, there is no stond or impediment in the wit, but may be wrought out by fit studies; like as diseases of the body, may have appropriate exercises. Bowling is good for the stone and reins; shooting for the lungs and breast; gentle walking for the stomach; riding for the head; and the like. So if a man's wit be wandering, let him study the mathematics; for in demonstrations, if his wit be called away never so little, he must begin again. If his wit be not apt to distinguish or find differences, let him study the schoolmen; for they are *cymini sectores:* if he be not apt to beat over matters, and to call up one thing to prove and illustrate another, let him study the lawyers' cases. So every defect of the mind, may have a special receipt.

FOUR

Lifestyles of the Rich and Toga-ed

Lives of Plutarch

If I seem too tired and cranky to write this, it's because I've exhausted myself just lugging this book around. It fell off the shelf as I tugged on it, but I think the dog will be okay, just got the bejabbers scared out of him.

The *Lives* of Plutarch are an amazing body of work, not least of which is that he has cranked out, in this volume alone:

— biographies of fifteen famous Greeks and Romans

— five essays comparing different figures and

— ten essays and letters on different subjects ranging from the death of his baby daughter to why God takes so long to punish the wicked. (Here's a thought, maybe he was too busy trying to wade through this book!)

If I approached *The Lives* with more than the usual amount of trepidation, it had to do with more than just the size of the book. Plutarch is one of those really intimidating names. Whenever anyone a hundred years ago mentioned a Greek or Roman of any stature, Plutarch is who they quoted.[19] This is THE book that much of our knowledge (or

---

19. In fact, the medieval church listed Plutarch as one of the few pagans who would get into heaven despite not being Christian. Others included Plato and Socrates. It was awfully big of them, don't ya think?

at least assumptions) of the past is based on.

Shakespeare lifted Caesar and Antony right off these pages. Alexander the Great and... well after that you find all kinds of characters like Lycurgus and Themistocles that I suppose someone heard of once, but certainly aren't household names. Of course, Shakespeare didn't write plays about them, that was the Elizabethan equivalent of the biopic. You always remember the movie.

Quick: What was the name of the mathematician in *A Beautiful Mind?* Right—John Nash. Bonus points: Name three other mathematicians...ever... I'll wait.

I don't know if Plutarch was the first, but he was certainly one of the first, to write biographies that weren't either long poems paid for by the person in question to make them look good, or outright lies to make the story better. I also found out, as I ploughed through this, that he did something more, something that is now commonplace but must have been incredibly innovative for the time—comparative history.

He wrote a number of essays comparing Greeks and Romans in different areas of expertise: the orators Demosthenes and Cicero, the generals Pericles and Fabius Maximus, the leadership of Demetrius and Marcus Antonius, all are examined by comparing their actions side by side and judgment passed down from the writer.

In short, I should have been more excited about the prospects for this book. Biography has always fascinated me—what people did and why they did it—if we can ever determine that for sure. As someone who's read more than his share of biographies, I should have been chomping to get at this one; Plutarch is the great-great-great granddaddy of all biographers. But this book sat on the shelf daring me to tackle it. It's a big'un, and extra bonus points to anyone who can say "Demosthenes, the father of Demosthenes, said Theopompus of Chios..." without tearing a ligament in their tongue and developing a permanent tic and stutter.

It doesn't help at all that I had either never heard of the first eight names on the list, or had only the vaguest inkling of who they were.

I mean, come on, Numa Pompilius?[20] Who wasn't waiting for the definitive biography of HIM?

It didn't take me long to get into it, though. To the modern reader the going is slow but not as bad as I thought it would be. That sounds like damning with faint praise but I expected sanitized, almost hagiographic accounts of their lives. What Plutarch wrote was remarkably balanced. Certainly by the standards of today's writers it's pretty tame stuff, but it doesn't shrink from laying it all on the line.

The lives of Marcus Antonius (Marc Antony of Shakespearean fame) and Demetrius (a Greek dictator and all around tough guy) are compared basically to show who was the biggest heel. This is a tough call by the way. Demetrius was the son of a king, and brutal in his dealing with his enemies. Marcus Antonius rose from the middle class to usurp the throne of the largest empire in the world. Both had scandalous love affairs and both careers ended in shame and ruin. Now Plutarch is a Stoic by nature and decides at the end that Antonius (while the bigger all around rat) has a more honorable death because he killed himself before being taken prisoner, while Demetrius died in prison, fat, broken and more than a little insane.

In most of these comparisons, to be sure, the Greeks come off as the better bunch. Read between the lines and you come to see that most of that is because as a Roman, and born about the year A.D. 1, many of the people he wrote about were still fresh in the public's memory. Cicero had just been killed, the bloody civil wars of Caesar, Brutus, and Antony still echoed in the halls of the Senate. Those characters were more real, and far less idealized than the Greeks, who had the good sense to be dead for a few hundred years and thus easier to keep on their pedestal. It was easy to feel good about Alexander kicking the holy falafels out of the Persians, the streets of Rome weren't filled with

---

20. I know you're dying to know. He was the first appointed king of Rome after its founding by Romulus. Plutarch used him as the example of how to rule without using force. Don't you feel smarter already?

refugees from Artemesia and Piraeus.[21] On the other hand, they were teeming with Gauls and Goths and all kinds of strange people, reminders that Roman armies were a long way from home and messing in a lot of other folks' business. If that sounds familiar, it should.

As biography, it does read a bit stilted, and the lack of gory detail does require some mental paint by numbers to make it real, but the lives are chosen for their instructive purposes: What happens to tyrants? What is the role of the orator in society? Plutarch puts the questions to us through the ages, and I have to wonder if many of our current crop of leaders and would-be historical figures have made this assigned reading.

This instructive tone might put people off, because it sure isn't Kitty Kelly, although his account of Cleopatra and Antonius' wild affair comes pretty close if you can use enough mental Ajax to scrub the memory of Elizabeth Taylor and Richard Burton from your cortex.

A quick digression: I believe our fear of, and intimidation by, the Romans stems from the movies and the fact that they are all played by people with thick upper-class English accents. Last time I checked Rome was in Italy, and the Romans invaded Britain, not the other way around. Latin politics makes a lot more sense if you think of them less as Lawrence Olivier or Peter Ustinov and more as Tony Soprano. Al Pacino as Marc Antony makes a lot more sense historically... I would love to hear him do the speech in Julius Caesar... "Cassius is out of order, Brutus is out of order, this whole Funeral's out of order...." And it all makes a lot more sense.

I read through the *Lives,* slowly gaining momentum. It's more exciting than I expected it to be, and certainly there is some degree of humanity to these people, but there was something a little odd about them. It took a while to bubble to the surface, but finally it hit me: These books were set up with the sole purpose of instruction. We are supposed to learn something from these people. Emulate their greatness, avoid

---

21. Battles the Greeks fought against the Persians in what is now Iraq. The thing about reading enough history is the annoying sense of déjà vu one feels. How many times are they going to fight over the same pieces of ground?

their mistakes do not pass Go, do not collect $200.

When was the last time someone wrote a biography with that agenda? When was the last time you read something that set out to hold another human being as a role model to be consciously emulated?

Of course, who does our generation have to hold up? Even the best of us is still—well—us. We have reached the time where the people leading the country are the people we went to college with. Sleep well.

This really hit home when I found out a girl I dated the summer between high school and college is now the Canadian Consul General to Guadalajara, Mexico. She is a bright woman, and I wish her nothing but the best, but the notion of a woman who once or twice played tonsil-hockey with me on Tsawassen beach being in charge of foreign policy is enough to give one a sleepless night or two.[22] On the other hand, the fact that I only got to second base tells me she is open to negotiation but ready to stand firm, so maybe it's not such a stretch after all.

Still, it does give one pause to think that the next wave of folks with access to the treasury and The Button are the same folks we went to college with. Consider their qualifications:

- Think Plutarch is Mickey's dog
- Don't speak a second language
- Think Ralph Nader is a radical
- Can't locate Kazakhstan on a map but can make a hell of a bong out of tin foil and a mango
- Can tell you the name of all the folks on Gilligan's Island but can't name three cabinet members

We also have too high a level of irony in our diet. We know too much and it's too hard to get past stuff to admire anyone. Think about it: Who was the last person our generation revered?

- Kennedy is the guy who banged Marilyn and hung with gangsters
- Gandhi drank his own urine and had some strange

---

22. Fortunately, it's Canadian foreign policy so how much harm can it really do? Still.....

interaction with young girls. He may have been father of
a country, but his kids were less impressed with his gifts
- FDR? Maybe, if you get past the affair with his secretary,
his odd relationship with Eleanor and his complete
disregard for the constitution
- Lincoln?

Okay. We have to go back 130 years before we find a leader we can unabashedly hold up without a wink.

Maybe it's (and I hesitate to go here, not because I risk offending someone but because the term makes me gag) the post-modernist approach to history. There is no truth. Everything is relative to who you are and where you come from. The fact that nothing is ever really true, means nothing is worthy of admiration. The acts or thoughts of someone are so dependant on their context that ultimately, it's all futile.

You can't admire Thomas Jefferson's words or the fact that what he helped set in motion is pretty impressive because he owned slaves. The fact that it was a legal institution into which he was born—and felt ambivalent about most of his life—is irrelevant. Everything he did is irrelevant. Bring on the next Dead White Male.

On the other hand, you can't hold people of another group to the same standard. Jesse Jackson can engage in extramarital affairs, break laws regarding contact with enemy nations, and no one can call him on it or we're just racist, sexist, put the "ist" of your choice here, idiots.

The result is that nothing is ultimately accepted as true and cynicism sets in. In one way this is a very good thing; we are far less likely to follow blindly someone whose warts we know. On the other hand, how do you create positive role models or unifying cultural icons? Either you learn to accept people warts and all, or there are a lot of babies and bathwater going out the window together. The chore is to make conscious decisions based on careful analysis. I know, I know, but that's all there is to it so quit whining.

We are all the products of the stories we're told, and for everyone to be told the same stories takes a huge degree of cooperation bordering on the collusive. George Washington and the cherry tree is a complete fabrication, but we all heard the story and it served its purpose. Of course, now we know it's not true—he had one of his ill-treated slaves do it for him and turn it into railway ties to exploit the Chinese. Lincoln walking through the snow to return a nickel, don't forget Santa Claus, the Tooth Fairy and Enron annual reports—are all tales for children and totally discredited by the folks of our generation. But what has replaced them except cynicism and dueling agendae?

What happens when a country no longer shares the same stories? When one person's hero is another person's bogeyman? Martin Luther King is a saint, nope he was a womanizing grandstander. Cesar Chavez led a noble fight for human dignity, unless he was a strong-arming dictator.

It must have been easier when everyone just believed Plutarch and took it from there. He actually addresses this issue in his essay on Pericles. He says,

> "In other fields, admiration of the deed is not instantly followed by an impulse to perform it. On the contrary, we are often charmed with a piece of work but look down on the workman. In the case of dyes and perfumes, for instance, we enjoy them but think of dyers and perfumers as servile and vulgar people..."

In other words, admiring someone or their work doesn't mean you accept everything about them. In the case of history that means actually thinking critically, and that is a ton of work.

It's easier to think of Jefferson as either a genius saint or a racist monster. To separate the good from the bad takes more mental gold-panning than most of us are prepared to indulge in.

So why read history? According to Caesar,[23] the reason is simple:

---

23. According to Plutarch, that is. See how this can make you crazy? You need to read history with enough grains of salt to cause a stroke.

"Not through imitating only does it mold the beholder's character—but through a study of great deeds he arrives at a purpose in life."

Plutarch is full of great deeds by men of questionable moral fiber:

- Fabius Maximus fights Hannibal and saves Rome despite questionable politics
- Themistocles raw ambition makes him a hero against the Persians, but he winds up working for them in the end, broken and chased out of Athens
- Gaius Marcus Coriloanus discovers that "He did not know that one who is undertaking public office must, above all, avoid self-will, which Plato calls the Housemate of Solitude, and must mingle with men and enjoy taking their buffeting, even though to some that attitude seems undignified." Are you reading this Messrs. Bush, Condit, Clinton and all?

History, it seems to me, has not changed its function over the years. It is not designed to provide answers, but it does teach us the questions to ask. The bear is, we're then expected to live by the answers.

Don't believe me? Plutarch says: "If we fail to think and live as we ought, we cannot in justice blame the smallness of our native city, but ourselves."

So there.

Without a doubt, Plutarch moves to the head of the valuable things I've read during this run. Even modern biography like *Warriors of God*, by James Reston (a mighty good book to my way of thinking) is more than a good read. If you take the time to examine the statements it makes and use a truly critical, as opposed to cynical, eye, the reading is that much more satisfying.

This one is a keeper.

COMPARISON OF DEMOSTHENES AND CICERO
— Plutarch, 75 A.C.E. (translation by John Dryden)

These are the most memorable circumstances recorded in history of Demosthenes and Cicero which have come to our knowledge. But omitting an exact comparison of their respective faculties in speaking, yet thus much seems fit to be said; that Demosthenes, to make himself a master in rhetoric, applied all the faculties he had, natural or acquired, wholly that way that he far surpassed in force and strength of eloquence all his contemporaries in political and judicial speaking, in grandeur and majesty all the panegyrical orators, and in accuracy and science all the logicians and rhetoricians of his day; that Cicero was highly educated, and by his diligent study became a most accomplished general scholar in all these branches, having left behind him numerous philosophical treatises of his own on Academic principles as, indeed, even in his written speeches, both political and judicial, we see him continually trying to show his learning by the way.

And one may discover the different temper of each of them in their speeches. For Demosthenes's oratory was without all embellishment and jesting, wholly composed for real effect and seriousness; not smelling of the lamp, as Pytheas scoffingly said, but of the temperance, thoughtfulness, austerity, and grave earnestness of his temper. Whereas Cicero's love of mockery often ran him into scurrility; and in his love of laughing away serious arguments in judicial cases by jests and facetious remarks, with a view to the advantage of his clients, he paid too little regard to what was decent: saying, for example, in his defense of Caelius, that he had done no absurd thing in such plenty and affluence to indulge himself in pleasures, it being a kind of madness not to enjoy the things we possess, especially since the most eminent philosophers have asserted pleasures to be the chiefest good.

So also we are told that when Cicero, being consul, undertook the defence of Murena against Cato's prosecution, by way of bantering Cato, he made a long series of jokes upon the absurd paradoxes, as they are called, of the Stoic set; so that a loud laughter passing from the crowd to the judges, Cato, with a quiet smile, said to those that sat next him, "My friends, what an amusing consul we have."

And, indeed, Cicero was by natural temper very much disposed to mirth and pleasantry, and always appeared with a smiling and serene countenance. But Demosthenes had constant care and thoughtfulness in his look, and a serious anxiety, which he seldom, if ever, laid aside; and therefore, was accounted by his enemies, as he himself confessed, morose and ill-mannered.

Also, it is very evident, out of their several writings, that Demosthenes never touched upon his own praises but decently and without offence when there was need of it and for some weightier end; but upon other occasions modestly and sparingly. But Cicero's immeasurable boasting of himself in his orations argues him guilty of an uncontrollable appetite for distinction, his cry being evermore that arms should give place to the gown, and the soldier's laurel to the tongue. And at last we find him extolling not only his deeds and actions, but his orations also, as well those that were only spoken, as those that were published; as if he were engaged in a boyish trial of skill, who should speak best, with the rhetoricians, Isocrates and Anaximenes, not as one who could claim the task to guide and instruct the Roman nation, the "Soldier full-armed, terrific to the foe."

It is necessary, indeed, for a political leader to be an able speaker; but it is an ignoble thing for any man to admire and relish the glory of his own eloquence. And, in this matter, Demosthenes had a more than ordinary gravity and magnificence of mind, accounting his talent in speaking nothing more than a mere accomplishment and matter of practice, the success of which must depend greatly on the good-will and candour of his hearers, and regarding those who pride themselves on such accounts to be men of a low and petty disposition.

The power of persuading and governing the people did, indeed, equally belong to both, so that those who had armies and camps at command stood in need of their assistance; as Charas, Diopithes, and Leosthenes of Demosthenes, Pompey and young Caesar of Cicero's, as the latter himself admits in his Memoirs addressed to Agrippa and Maecenas. But what are thought and commonly said most to demonstrate and try the tempers of men, namely, authority and place, by moving every passion, and discovering every frailty, these are things which Demosthenes never received; nor was he ever in a position to give such proof of himself, having never obtained any eminent office, nor led any of those armies into the field against Philip which he raised by his eloquence. Cicero, on the other hand, was sent quaestor into Sicily, and proconsul into Cilicia and Cappadocia, at a time when avarice was at the height, and the commanders and governors who were employed abroad, as though they thought it a mean thing to steal, set themselves to seize by open force; so that it seemed no heinous matter to take bribes, but he that did it most moderately was in good esteem. And yet he, at this time, gave the most abundant proofs alike of his contempt of riches and of his humanity and good-nature. And at Rome, when he was created consul in name, but indeed received sovereign and dictatorial authority against Catiline and his conspirators, he attested the truth of Plato's prediction, that then the miseries of states would be at an end when, by a happy fortune, supreme power, wisdom, and justice should be united in one.

FIVE

If George W. Were Roman

Discourses of Cicero

Well, it was bound to happen sooner or later. I finally found a book I couldn't care less about. *The Discourses of Cicero* was not the most scintillating thing I've read lately. Okay, I've read cereal boxes with more drama—it's hard to beat the addition of Niacin for pulse-pounding action. It's doubly disappointing since Plutarch made Cicero's life sound so dramatic and fascinating.[24] After all, he was a politician and political schemer who eventually was assassinated for backing the wrong horse.

A letter he wrote called "Of Duty" should have tipped me off. To his son he wrote:

> "...by reading my books you will certainly increase your command of the Latin language. I do not wish you to think I am boasting. In knowledge of philosophy there are many better than I, but I feel justified in claiming the special proficiency of an orator in speaking suitably, clearly and gracefully for I have devoted my life to the study of that art."

---

24. It's not unusual for the book of someone's life to be more interesting than the person themselves or their work. See anything written about Truman Capote or Andy Warhol.

Well, since I sure wasn't reading them in Latin, I wasn't going to get much value there, and he freely admits there are better philosophers, so he's already starting behind the eight ball.

Now, to be fair, Cicero was an orator; his words were meant to be heard, and in Latin no less. He was also a lawyer, which is exactly the problem with this book. Most of this book is nothing more than glorified court transcripts. I don't know who Marcus Caelius was, but even if his trial were the Simpson affair of his generation, it lacks something on the written page.

As a character, Cicero was worth finding out about. He was a major supporter of Marcus Antonius, or Marc Antony if you're a Shakespeare buff. Given the full contact politics of Rome, you were pretty much in trouble no matter which way you leaned, and Cicero led with his chin.

Near as I can figure, our esteem for Marc Antony depends largely on how you feel about his fling with Cleopatra. The eloquent eulogy in *Julius Caesar* was not so much honest grief for a fallen friend than a cynical attempt to put himself in position to rule Rome. Antonius was a full-blown gangster. If you liked him, picture Robert De Niro. If you didn't, he's played by Joe Pesci.

The role of orator in our society has been completely debased. We don't value those who speak eloquently; in fact, poetic language is often mocked. Speeches, rather than being preserved for posterity are snipped into ten-second clips for CNN or put in their entirety on CSPAN. Either way, they don't get heard.

There certainly have been great speeches given. "A day which will live in infamy" is a fabulous phrase, but it was delivered on radio. At a time of national crisis now, we have George W. knitting his brow and saying "We will not tire, we will not falter, and we will not fail." While he gets major points for alliterations (a sure-fire rhetorical tool) and I have no doubt he is sincere, it lacks something.

It smacks of a committee of speech writers saying, "Hey, let's run this up the flagpole and see who salutes it." It's careful. It was delivered by a man completely uncomfortable with large gestures. It was designed for a television audience, delivered to a camera that multiplies the impact of each gesture yet still seemed barely adequate.

Make no mistake, on that Tuesday afternoon I wanted gestures, as big and bold as I could get them. I wanted a Churchill, "All we have to offer are blood, sweat, toil and tears."

I wanted the fire of Henry V in his St. Swithin's Day speech. Hell, I'd have settled for Bill Pullman in his *Independence Day* speech.

Instead, we got a careful, telegenically measured response from a man who may be a good manager, but is clearly no orator. I couldn't help but wonder how those same words in the mouth of Bill Clinton would have sounded.

There was a man who understood the power of oratory. Until his credibility landed in a heap with his underwear, he could charm the very birds out of the trees. He could deliver one heck of a speech, and I think I know why.

Clinton was, as I was, raised on sermons. Not just any sermon, mind you, but Baptist sermons. He, like I did, watched what the good preachers could do to a room. We'll put aside for a moment the question of content or intention. Intellectually, logically and factually they may be badly flawed—even dangerously so—but they could burn that mother down when the need arose.

Watching the Pentecostal preacher Jimmy Swaggart work a stage in Maple Leaf Gardens in Toronto was a life-changing experience. He transfixed an entire hockey arena full of people, driving them to foot stomping, tongue—speaking, spirit—dancing ecstasy. I couldn't help but feel the power.

Did I know at that time he was a hypocrite and a cheat? Yup. Did it matter at that moment? Nope. Not a whit.

His speech was not designed to appeal to the brain. It was spirit talking to spirit, and that's when oratory really shines. It's that perfect blend of words, gestures, the person delivering it, and the audience.

Cicero's words on paper cannot possibly give me the full impact of what he must have been like; in fact, it's pretty much a pale reflection. He was an orator and I'd have to hear his voice, even see him work it to know how good he was.

You have to have the entire package, visual, verbal, and vocal in order to really get the full impact of a message. One of the most quoted (and usually inaccurately) statistics of the last thirty years was the Mehrabian study out of UCLA. It said, in part, that the impact of a message is

- 63% visual (what the audience sees)
- 30% vocal (what they hear and perceive in your voice)
- 7% verbal (what it is you actually say)

What it seems to say is that *what* you say doesn't nearly matter as much as how you look saying it. That's the way it's usually presented, but it's not the entire message. That's the impact of a message when there is a disconnection between what they see and hear. If the message and the messenger are in accord, you get Churchill, Lincoln, and Gandhi. When it doesn't—when what people see overpowers the message itself—you get Hitler, Mussolini, and Christina Aguilera.

One of my favorite examples of this is Kennedy's Berlin Wall speech. When he said *"Ich bin ein Berliner."* The world went crazy. He was a Berliner, by golly, and he was going to stand tall. Kruschev better put that shoe back on his foot and get running. One problem:

Ich bin Berliner means I'm a Berliner.

Ich bin ein Berliner means I am a doughnut. What was he gonna do, spread a sticky glaze all over Check Point Charlie till the Russians caved in?

It didn't seem to matter much to people at the time, it was a good speech delivered well, and they heard what they wanted to hear. It is a pretty elegant example if I do say so myself.

I'm another pretty good example, now that I think about it. All my life I've gotten credit for being way smarter than I really am by being able to speak confidently. Whether it was a grammar school assembly or a smoky nightclub, just the fact that I could stand up and speak coherently gave people the impression that I knew what I was talking about. Use big words, quote someone they've never read so they can't bust you on it, et voila: instant credibility. More fool them.

My dirty little secret, of course, is that the really smart people were in the back of the class too busy actually doing the work to worry about presenting it. In addition, it's a fairly unnatural act to speak in public, and most people don't do it well, so the tendency is to give those of us who can do it way more credit than we deserve.

I've made a pretty good living over the years teaching people to present in public. Most people think it's because I can do it, I can teach it. That's not necessarily the case. The reason I got into training was because a thought occurred to me in the wee small hours of a dark unemployed night: Is it easier to teach someone who knows something to present it, or is it easier to teach a good presenter the subject matter?

The fact of the matter is, as everyone from Demosthenes to Cicero to good old Dr. Mehrabian and Billy Crystal will tell you, it's more important to look good than to be good. That would seem to give the edge to the "good presenter" argument. The difference is, that the tricks of good presenting are fairly easily identified and taught. They can be coached and improved. Bad presenters can become, if not great, at least competent.

On the other hand, dumb is dumb, and someone who doesn't know their stuff but has all the tools to appear knowledgeable is just a danger to themselves and everyone who works for them. I'll bet those Andersen accountants at Enron could PowerPoint their butts off.

It's obvious that medieval Italy didn't have political consultants, or Dante would have had a tenth level of hell reserved for that bunch.

Believe me, we'll all sleep better knowing I'm trying to help smart people be better at their job, and not helping dumb people be better at whatever it is dumb people do well.

Back in the day, of course, it appears such efforts were better rewarded. Demosthenes, the Greek orator, worked hard at becoming the known world's greatest speechifier. According to Plutarch he started talking with a mouth of pebbles to improve his enunciation, and practiced his speeches on a cliff shouting into the wind, to boost his lung power and volume. That's dedication. I can't get people to turn off their Blackberries[25] in class.

As to his involvement in politics, I have no idea whether Cicero was right or wrong, I only know that his support of Marcus Antonius got him arrested and ultimately killed. It doesn't exactly make you want to run out and put a lawn sign out during the primaries, if you know what I mean.

This is Cicero's speech to the people: Antony is back in power and Cicero is once again out of jail and back at his work. Keep in mind it was said in Latin, so I have no idea if it sounded as wordy as it does here. I mean, it's no "If the glove doesn't fit you must acquit" or anything....

TO THE CITIZENS AFTER HIS RETURN
— Cicero

[1] That which I requested in my prayers of the all-good and all-powerful Jupiter, and the rest of the immortal gods, O Romans, at the time when I devoted myself and my fortunes in defense of your safety, and tranquility, and concord,—namely, that if I had at any time preferred my own interests to your safety, I might find that punishment, which I was then encountering of my own accord, everlasting; but that if I had done those things which I had done out of an honest desire to preserve the state, and if I had undertaken that miserable journey on which I was then setting out for the sake of ensuring your safety, in order that the hatred which wicked and audacious

---

25. Those annoying little text message thingies that seem to be everywhere but in my hands; whether due to technophobia or lack of funds is for others to determine.

men had long since conceived and entertained against the republic and against all good men, might break upon me alone, rather than on every virtuous man, and on the entire republic—if I say these were my feelings towards you and towards your children, that in that case, a recollection of me, a pity and regret for me should, at some time or other come upon you and the conscript fathers, and all Italy, I now rejoice above all things that that request is heard that I am bound to perform all that I then vowed, by the judgment of the immortal gods,—by the testimony of the senate by the unanimous consent of all Italy,—by the confession of my enemies,—by your godlike and never-to-be-forgotten kindness, O citizens of Rome.[26]

[2] For although there is nothing more to be wished for by man than prosperous, equal, continual good-fortune in life, flowing on in a prosperous course, without any misadventure; still, if all my life had been tranquil and peaceful, I should have been deprived of the incredible and almost heavenly delight and happiness which I now enjoy through your kindness. What sweeter thing has been given to the race of man, or to each individual, by nature, than his own children? To me especially, mine, on account of my affectionate nature, and on account of their own excellent qualities, are dearer to me than my life. And yet I did not feel that pleasure when they were born, that I feel now when they are restored to me.[27]

[3] Nothing was ever more acceptable to any one, than my brother is to me. I was not so aware of this when I enjoyed his society, as I became when I was deprived of it, and after you again restored me to him and him to me. His own private estate is a pleasure to every one. The relics of my fortune, which I have recovered, give me now greater delight than they used to give when they were unimpaired. Friendship, familiar intercourse,

---

26. Whew! At this point, how many people do you think were reconsidering their decision to let him back?

27. See, you don't know what you got till it's gone. And I always thought Joni Mitchell was an original....

acquaintance with my neighbors, the dependence of one's clients on one, even games and days of festival, are things the delights of which I have learnt to appreciate better by being deprived of them than I did while I was enjoying them.

[4] And honor, dignity, my rank and order, and, above all, your kindness, although they at all times appeared to me most splendid possessions, yet, now that they are recovered, after having been lost, they appear more bright than if they had never been hidden from my sight. And as for my country, O ye immortal gods, it is scarcely possible to express how dear, how delightful it is to me. How great is the beauty of Italy! How renowned are its cities! How varied are the enchantments of its scenery! What lands, what crops are here! How noble is the splendour of this city, and the civilization of its citizens, and the dignity of the republic, and your majesty, O people of Rome! Even of old, no one took greater delight in all those things than I did. But as good health is more welcome to those who are just recovered from a severe illness than to those who have never been sick, so all those things, now that they have been once missed, delight me more than they did when enjoyed without interruption.

One last thought: It's either ironic or just plain sick coincidence that the most mob-ridden town in Illinois (a not inconsiderable achievement) is named after an Italian lawyer. Draw your own conclusions.

SIX

Interlude #1

The Universe Unfolds

This is as good a time as any to take stock of where I am at in my slog through time. I say this for two reasons:

1. I've completed five books, four of which I thought were worth reading
2. Something happened today which I can't explain but makes perfect sense if you believe in omens, which I'm not sure I do

First a quick status report: five down, a bunch to go. I'm grouping them as Worth It (Epictetus, Bacon, Browning), Really Worth It (my new main man, Plutarch) and Well, Checked That One Off the List. Sorry, Cicero, you are the Weakest Link—good-bye.

I'm not finding the reading as hard as I thought I would. True, if I were trying to speed-read this stuff I'd probably have spun right off the page and smacked into a wall causing permanent damage, but since I'm intentionally taking my time it's not too bad. I think for a lot of people my age it would be more difficult, especially Bacon, with the *thous* and *arts*. I like it and I think I know the reason.

Anyone raised in Sunday school in the '60s or '70s will have a much easier time reading these books than someone who wasn't. It's not that we're that much smarter than anyone else, we just had good training. The King James Bible, written in the 1600s, taught us our "Thees and Thous" so it's not so strange seeing them on the page.

I am going to make a confession here: I still use my King James version. I don't like modern translations of the Bible; they lack poetry and the language is too informal. I know they say that the King James is politically incorrect and makes God too hard to reach. Tough. He's an important guy, he should be tough to reach. How impressive would Bill Gates be if anyone could just ring him up to chat? Heck, I can't even get close to Sammy Sosa on autograph day at Wrigley Field, and he didn't create the world in seven days.

Personally, a little mystery and awe is important. I don't think we can even really grasp what or who God is, and making him "personal" and "relevant" smacks of more than a little hubris on our part. If salvation is in that book (and I'm prepared to grant you that if you'll grant there might be others too) we should probably have to work a little bit for it.

And let's face it, as art these new translations leave a little to be desired. There's something majestic about the original Christmas story in Luke: "Shepherds abiding in the fields, keeping watch o'er their flocks by night, and Lo…" It works for me. I just like the ring of it more than in the New- Living- Standard- Revised- Modern- Good- News Edition: "There were shepherds in the fields with their sheep and suddenly angels appeared…" or the newest version: "Shepherds were chilling when dudes in white suddenly showed up…"

The reason I feel this way, I'm a bit embarrassed to admit, is that I don't really buy the whole story in any version. I'll give you the baby. In a generous mood I might give you the stable. Beyond that I think we're in awfully deep water. The real reason I prefer the older version is more cynical than theological: If you're going to tell me a story, make it a good one and dress it up. The more you try to convince me it's true, the harder I'll scrutinize it and the less I'll believe you. Don't even get me started on Genesis.

I also want to clarify that when I say I "use" the King James, honesty demands that I also admit that it doesn't get used very often, except when I'm looking for a good quote or trying to prove a point. A biblical scholar I'm not.

Here's the point I'm driving to: If you can wade through all the begats, whithers and any of the minor prophets, Bacon, Plutarch, and the boys are no big challenge.

So I'm generally feeling pretty good about myself. I have managed to begin this project and have a pretty good head of steam going. I have found quotes and resources I never new existed (at least one of which has turned up in a company newsletter), have gotten intrigued by the Stoics, and I'm actually looking forward to reading Marcus Aurelius to find out more.

I've mentioned this before, but the weirdest thing is happening. In every book I've read so far (even Cicero to give him his due) there is at least one thing that leaps out at me. It seems to fit exactly what I'm going through either at work or at Casa Turmel. Epictetus has cheered me up, Bacon has inspired me, and Plutarch put a whole lot of stuff in perspective.[28]

Why hasn't anyone told me this before? I feel like I want to tell someone about what I'm doing here. What I'm beginning to suspect is that nobody gives a rat's butt. I tried to explain to The Duchess why Bacon still mattered, and she gave me the same look I got when I tried to explain the infield fly rule to her. Her Serene Highness is not overly impressed by anything not endorsed by the Olsen Twins.

And that brings me up to this morning and point number two. When you ask questions of the universe, you'd best be prepared for an answer. I'm sure I missed a lot of them in my lifetime, but today I listened.

I'm flying from Chicago to Boston, exactly one month after

---

28. Let's face it. After disembowelings, kidnappings and asps, you haven't' really had a bad day at work like some of the folks Plutarch talks about. When was the last time anyone in your company was actually assassinated or had their kids killed for not meeting month end?

September 11. I am not nervous about flying, I think to myself, I'm not, I'm not, I'm not. I slide into my aisle seat and notice gratefully that the seat next to me is empty.

This is a good thing. While I'm a generally friendly person, I very rarely converse with fellow passengers.

First of all, I don't like to make the first move. I smile, nod, wait for the headsets and put the psychic cone of silence up around me.

I pull out my book Ken Wilber's "Theory of Everything," and settle in. Just as they are about to take off, and I'm ready to gleefully sacrifice a goat to whichever deity is in charge of providing empty seats next to you on the plane, one last person comes on board.

Youngish.

Male.

Three day's growth of beard.

Middle Eastern looking.

I feel my sphincter tighten perceptibly. It really puts on a full-court press when I realize there is only one empty seat in this part of the plane. No, no, no... I feel myself splitting in two. I try to convince myself that I'm really only upset because my elbow room just left, not because I could be sitting next to a terrorist. I try to reason with myself. Nobody who is planning to move quickly in order to commandeer a plane would ever take a middle seat. I've taken five minutes to get up and out to make a regulation pit stop.

Still, I can't help looking him up and down suspiciously. I smile grimly and nod as I get up to let him in. I'm proud of myself for resisting the urge to frisk him as he goes by. He nods back and plunks into his seat like he envies the dead. Staring straight ahead, not reading, not doing anything, just staring straight ahead. Chicago to Boston is a little over two hours. I get the sinking feeling it could feel like a day and a half before we land.

My neighbor says nothing for the first half hour, just gazes straight ahead blankly. I try to focus on my book, but it's almost impossible to decipher heavy philosophical thought when you are wondering if the guy next to you has C-4 lining his jockey shorts.

Finally the flight attendant comes by with the coffee. He snaps out of whatever Jihad-inspired trance I presume him to be in and he looks at her. "Coffee, please," he asks politely. I pass the coffee along to him with what I hope is my best I-really-sympathize-with-the-Palestinians smile. He nods and gives me a nod.

"Is that a good book?" He points to the Wilber on my tray. He speaks in a very clipped, classy British accent, and I reduce the odds of his carrying a box cutter by about fifty percent. I try not to choke on my coffee.

"Wilber. Do you know him?"

"No, but I've been reading the back cover."

I grin. That's how I spy on people too, by trying to figure out what kind of people they are by the book they're reading. The thought that someone would draw conclusions about me that way should scare me, but for once this isn't something I'm embarrassed to be caught reading.

"It sounds like something I'd be interested in reading." And the darnedest thing happens: He begins to speak to me…

Turns out he's a nuclear cardiologist in Chicago to take a board exam to add to the seventeen or so letters after his name. He may be the single most educated person I've ever spoken to. I go from guilty suspicion to intellectual inferiority in about 2.4 seconds.

His basset-brown eyes focus on me seriously as we discuss the notion that at their core, most religions say the same thing about who or what God might be and what we need to do about it. I mutter some bad translation of what the book in my hand says and he nods enthusiastically.

"You know, the more science I learn, the more I realize there is still something missing. We are finding all about the *how* things work, and none of the *why*." As I sit listening to him, I'm amazed to realize that this person who has more education than I and the nearest four members of the Turmel family, is asking the same questions I am.

"Did you know," he says apropos of absolutely nothing, "that when I was doing my residency there was a study at—I think it's the University of San Francisco—about the power of prayer. It turns out that people who are prayed for recover at a thirty percent faster rate than people who aren't. All the medicine I've studied can't explain that. If prayer were a drug, it would get FDA approval and the medical establishment doesn't know what to do about that."

I ask him to tell me more, fascinated. It's not the information he shares with me, although that's interesting enough, lord knows. It's the tone in his voice, the feeling of excitement that he thought he was going somewhere no one else is going only to discover there is someone else heading the same way.

I offer my own suspicion that at the core of all religion is the same truth if you can cut through the allegory and ritual to the nuggets.

His smile fades just a bit, as if trying to figure out how I'd just read his mind. "Do you know," he probes, "how I got interested in religion again? I read a book by Robert Schuller..."

Something in what a Christian preacher said about God's love had sent my new friend back to his own roots in India, to read the ancient Islamic and Hindu writers. He couldn't buy Christianity—it was too foreign to him and, frankly, Christians hadn't exactly endeared themselves to him in the past—but there was something there he might find in his own culture, simply because it made more sense to him. "I don't know if you can relate to this," he said shyly, "but I felt the need to see if something in my own culture was worth reading, if it said the same thing. I can't explain it, but it's like there's something there if I just look hard enough."

"You probably think I'm crazy," he says finally.

I suppose he thinks that because I have this stupid grin on my face. "Not at all," I say, struggling for the right words. "It's just that I'm kind of doing the same thing."

Slowly, I tell him about my little journal project. How I'm finding strange solace in the Greeks and Romans and medieval writers I'm discovering. My search through the Dead White Males matches almost exactly his picking through the Dead Brown ones. All the reading, he says, he should have done in school but didn't.

We are on approach to Logan airport when we share things we've read lately that the other should read. I tell him about Ken Wilber, Teillhard de Chardin, and Plutarch. He tells me about the Sufi poets Rumi and El-Haffiz.

In less than an hour I have told him more about where I'm at philosophically than I've told my wife. He is the first living person to know I'm keeping a journal, and of what. "I'd be interested in seeing what you wrote," he offers. Well, maybe not, since at the moment he thinks I'm a reasonably intelligent person. If he saw what I was scribbling he'd probably change his mind awfully quick—and who cares what I think anyway.

Except he did seem to care. It made him awfully happy to discover that at least one other human was asking the same questions, and fumbling for the same answers in the same way. I wonder for a moment if anyone else would be interested in it. I know I'd like to see what he was coming up with.

All too soon it's "seat backs and trays to the upright position." The plane lands and the moment passes. We get separated in the usual crush of people at the back of the plane who believe standing in the aisle the moment the plane lands will magically get them off the plane sooner.

We don't exchange cards or email addresses. I catch a quick glance of him at baggage claim and he disappears into the cool New England afternoon. We never shake hands or promise to stay in touch.

It feels important. Later in my hotel room I write the whole incident down in my journal; the first nonbook related entry. I don't know why but this total stranger has given me even more inspiration to continue.

What do you know? People way smarter than me are on the same groping, stumbling path through the past I am. Who knew?

I think his name was Nair, but I can't swear to it.

SEVEN

God, Dracula, and Crazy Horse Mountain

Poems of John Milton

> ...he who would not be frustrate of his hope
> to write well hereafter in laudable things, ought
> himself to be a true poem, that is a composition
> and pattern of the best and honorablest things...
> —John Milton

Yeesh, no problem living up to this guy's standards.

Having gotten through Browning relatively unscathed, I wasn't as on my toes as I should have been to tackle Milton. This guy is everything you imagine a Dead White Guy to be—high-minded, stern, no sense of humor. There is nothing light or subtle about his work. Forget frothy poems of love or word play, romance is just not an important enough topic for John Milton. He wants to tackle nothing less than the very nature of good and evil, God and Satan.

I don't know what else you'd expect from someone who began to write poetry at the age of ten. I know Her Serene Highness is almost that age and writing poetry is nowhere on her radar screen. If I'd been writing poetry at ten I think I'd have gotten my butt kicked even worse than I did.

Unlike most child geniuses, Milton hung on to live to a ripe old age, which is most unprodigy-like. People who exhibit great talent early tend to burn out, as if everyone has only so much good stuff in them, and if it all comes out too early there's nothing left for the later years. Genius tends to burn brightly and flame out. Mediocrity hangs in there for the duration.

There's nothing mediocre about this guy Milton. His stuff reeks of serious art, which if you've never smelled it is a little like ammonia—you know it's good for you but can still give you an awful headache if you're around it for too long.

If you want to know why Milton matters, it's *Paradise Lost*. This massive poem is long on serious and short on logic that works for me. For example, did you know that Eve was blonde? I'm not nitpicking, here. This stuff matters, and I think I know why. Listen up because you won't find this little theory in any college textbook...

What makes Milton so important, for good or not depending on where you stand, is not his theological expertise but his sheer audacity. Milton made a heroic effort to do something every culture has attempted, and Western Europeans have done to an impressive degree: Make God both completely perfect and as much like us as possible. Assuming, of course, us is white, European and cranky.

His image of God, Satan, and the angels became the archetype for the next 200 years. This is the vision of Christianity that the enlightenment came to resent and that still makes me crazy when people take it literally.

The closest example I can come up with is Dracula.

Okay, granted, this one will take some explaining.

Vampire legends have been around for hundreds, if not thousands of years. They date back to the Egyptians or earlier. When Bram Stoker introduced Dracula, and especially thirty years later when the movie came out, suddenly everyone just knew what vampires were all about.

They were:

- cultured
- formally attired

- mildly Hungarian
- susceptible to crosses (which I get) and garlic (which to this day I don't understand)

Despite the best efforts of filmmakers, writers and Goth kids, that's still what our generation thinks vampires are. A slightly younger, more sexually ambiguous group might adhere to the Anne Rice school, but frankly the movie wasn't very good, and those vampires were French. You can't have a bloodsucking ghoul that surrenders at the first sign of a fight.

So, we now have this vision of God, angels, and Satan (the beautiful tempter devil, not the horns and pitchfork version)[29] which has stuck with us for the better part of 350 years. This is not without its pitfalls.

Much of Western society takes this poem more literally than it takes the source material. That's why since Milton says Eve is blonde, it makes sense that everyone else from that era is too; after all, in seventeenth century England you never even saw anyone with a tan, let alone a good Semitic swarthiness. We have done the Creator one better—we've created God in our own image, which is not a bad trick.

Not that it's terribly original. If you're Muslim, Allah will grant you paradise which involves numerous virgins at your disposal. If you're Hindu, eternity is full of music that doesn't sound like my idea of paradise, but then again the odds of me going there are more than a little remote, so more power to them.

So an Englishman created an Eden and a heaven that look amazingly like England and people who look like the residents of old Britannia. That image made the trip over on the Mayflower with the puritans and voila—the pictures of Jesus that most of us grew up with are paintings of the palest, straightest-haired, least Jewish-looking person ever to walk the byways of Galilee.

I suppose to many people that's a comfort, that they are more like

---

29. There isn't a lot of fire and brimstone in this poem either. Hell is not all that interesting to me. It's hot and smelly. Hey, I live in Chicago and the fact is that half the year I would kill to be there and the other half I already am.

God than "they" are—whoever they is. I don't feel that way at all. It's not political correctness, heaven knows,[30] but a deeper issue. As I read the story, I got the kind of knot I get in my stomach when I lock my keys in the car. Something was wrong, and I didn't know what it was but I knew it was big and I wouldn't like it when I figured out what it was.

It occurred to me as I read the story of the Serpent and the Garden what it was. I understood Satan's motivation—I'm more than comfortable with envy and feeling smarter than my boss, as career— threatening a feeling as that is. I even understood Adam and Eve giving in to the temptation. It was the picture of God that worried me.

He had created this one tree that Adam and Eve shouldn't eat. Not for any good reason, particularly, except as a test of their loyalty. That's the kind of bone-headed stunt I would do to teach my kid a lesson. That's hardly a comfort.

Let's just assume from now on I want a God that thinks NOTHING like I do. Face it, as a father I know that despite doing my very best I create a daily list of errors longer than baseball's infamous Chuck Knoblauch's. God the Father is not an image that comforted me once I got past the age of twelve and realized my father was not God.[31] If he were, the universe would have been created in just five days but held together with duct tape.

Here's an example of God acting like a human father:

> This said, he formed thee, Adam, thee O man
> Dust of the ground, and in thy nostrils breathed
> The breath of life; in his own image he
> Created thee, in the image of God
> Express and thou becamest a living soul.
> Male he created thee, but thy Consort

---

30. Actually, it might be geographical and historical correctness. I can handle prejudice if it's based on fact, but don't make stuff up or I'm liable to bust you on it. Not because I'm a better person than you, I just need to prove I'm smarter. How twisted is that?

31. Mary as a mother on the other hand, I can totally buy. Do you think she ever snapped at Jesus: "Hey, you left the door open. What were you born in a barn?"

> Female for race; then blessed mankind, and said,
> "Be fruitful, multiply, and fill the earth,
> Subdue it, and throughout dominion hold
> Over fish of the sea, and foul of the air
> And every living thing that moves on the earth."

Am I wrong or does that sound like a first class case of nepotism? Surely the animals that were already there had other plans until the boss brought his kid into the business.

Making God more personal does nothing to make me feel secure. The Greeks had gods that were like they were: melodramatic, quick to anger and so moody I can only assume they were in the clutches of a full-blown ouzo hangover. Interestingly, they weren't like the humans physically, as I have yet to see a statue of a Greek god with hair on its shoulders, or a Greek man who didn't.

Paradise Lost is not an easy read, either. It's a massive effort. It took years to write, not that much longer than it's taking to me to read it.

Apparently, the reading public at the time appreciated the effort because it was the first poem to be sold by subscription. People paid in advance for each installment with the same anticipation, supposedly, we hold to find out who gets voted off the island on *Survivor*.

I'm not one of those people who believes that in the old days people were that much smarter or more appreciative of art. Let's recall that this was a time without indoor plumbing, the Internet or Comedy Central. There weren't a lot of alternatives for ways to kill their leisure time.

I don't doubt that they appreciated it for the impressive task it was. First of all, the biblical story of both the creation and Lucifer's fall take place over about forty-seven verses spread throughout the Old Testament, plus a few hints in Revelations (which is about all you get of anything in Revelations). Milton manages to tell the same story in 290 pages of grinding, very labored poetry. It's an undertaking of Herculean proportions and regardless of my opinion, you gotta give Milton major points for effort. He gets extra bonus points for finishing the last half of it as he was going blind.

Recording the history of the cosmos and the workings of heaven plus the fall of man while remembering to capitalize the first word of every line is impressive enough. Then to do it with one hand (or eye as the case may be) tied behind your back is just this side of craziness.

I've always been impressed by people who dream big. I'm not talking "I'll be a millionaire by the time I'm thirty big," I'm talking "I'm gonna spend the rest of my life on this one project, no matter what anyone says" big.

Apparently Alexander the Great conquered every country he'd ever heard of, then cried because there were no new worlds to conquer. That's the kind of big I'm talking about.

Maybe the best example of this I've ever seen is in the Black Hills of South Dakota. There, mere miles from Mount Rushmore, sits the greatest tribute to monomania that's ever been my pleasure to witness. Crazy Horse Mountain may be the single most stupid-big, insanely focused, all-around American thing ever attempted.

For the uninitiated, it's the ultimate spit-in-the-eye to jingoism and overly ambitious white people. Rather than simply carve the faces of four presidents into the side of a mountain, we'll turn a whole mountain into a statue of our greatest chief—and on a horse no less. It's so big, that all four presidents on Rushmore will look like a pimple on Crazy Horse's chin.

First, simply as a gesture, you've got to dig it. Forget for a moment that they'll destroy a whole mountain in order to protest the white man desecrating sacred hills. The best part is it wasn't a Native American idea at all. It started over forty years ago in the brain of a slightly mad Polish immigrant. Is this a great country or what?

The topper for me, though, is he died years ago and his sons-in-law (as in more than one of them) are carrying on the work. It's one thing to follow your father-in-law into the family business when it's a restaurant or a CPA firm. It's another when that business entails hanging in a rope swing in thirty-five degree weather taking a jackhammer to a stone loincloth.

I can remember very clearly the first time I even heard about it. I was on a comedy tour in South Dakota and Nebraska. It was a bitterly cold April day, and we were laid over in Rapid City. We went to see Mt. Rushmore, which was fine but being Canadian I didn't experience whatever lump of patriotism was supposed to clog the throat. I also couldn't help thinking it would have been much cooler if James Mason actually had a house on the top of it, just like in *North by Northwest*.

On a lark we drove the extra miles to the site of Crazy Horse Mountain. The little public information site was empty except for my buddy and I. It was cold and misty, and we were hung over and cynical as hell.

From the warmth and safety of the office, I looked up at the mountain. There in white paint was the outline of where the statue would be and what it would look like. The size of it, the sheer audacity literally left me speechless.

I dropped a quarter in a telescope to watch a single person in a leather harness hanging by cables take a pneumatic hammer to the granite wall. From that distance there was no sound, just a small speck trying to carve a mountain into a conquered nation's last symbol of defiance. At that moment nothing seemed impossible.

I could still make it in show business.

Maybe I could get that green card after all.

I will find a good woman.

Well, two out of three ain't bad, even if they weren't in the order I expected. I didn't make it in show business, but to this day I remember the respect I felt for that crazy sculptor and everyone who was trying to keep the project alive. I developed a whole new appreciation for Open Mike Night.

As to John Milton, it was a lot of work, and I guess he gets points for sheer effort.

Here's the opening of *Paradise Lost*. It pretty much tells you what you're in for if you decide to tackle it...

PARADISE LOST
— John Milton, 1667

Book I
Of man's first disobedience, and the fruit
Of that forbidden tree whose mortal taste
Brought death into the world, and all our woe,
With loss of Eden, till one greater man
Restore us, and regain the blissful seat,
Sing, heavenly muse, that, on the secret top
Of Oreb, or of Sinai, didst inspire
That shepherd who first taught the chosen seed
In the beginning how the heavens and earth
Rose out of Chaos: Or, if Sion hill
Delight thee more, and Siloa's brook that flowed
Fast by the oracle of God; I thence
Invoke thy aid to my adventurous song,
That with no middle flight intends to soar
Above the Aonian mount, while it pursues
Things unattempted yet in prose or rhyme.[32]
And chiefly thou, O spirit, that dost prefer
Before all temples th' upright heart and pure,
Instruct me, for thou knowest; thou from the first
Wast present, and, with mighty wings outspread,
Dove-like satest brooding on the vast abyss,
And madest it pregnant: What in me is dark
Illumine, what is low raise and support;
That, to the height of this great argument,
I may assert eternal providence,

---

32. He got that right—this is a tall order.

And justify the ways of God to men.
Say first, for heaven hides nothing from thy view,
Nor the deep tract of hell, say first what cause
Moved our grand parents, in that happy state,
Favoured of Heaven so highly, to fall off
From their Creator, and transgress his will
For one restraint, lords of the World besides.
Who first seduced them to that foul revolt?
The infernal serpent; he it was[33] whose guile,
Stirred up with envy and revenge, deceived
The mother of mankind, what time his pride
Had cast him out from heaven, with all his host
Of rebel angels, by whose aid, aspiring
To set himself in glory above his peers,
He trusted to have equalled the Most High,
If he opposed, and with ambitious aim
Against the throne and monarchy of God,
Raised impious war in heaven and battle proud,
With vain attempt. Him the Almighty Power
Hurled headlong flaming from the ethereal sky,
With hideous ruin and combustion, down
To bottomless perdition, there to dwell
In adamantine chains and penal fire,
Who durst defy the Omnipotent to arms.
Nine times the space that measures day and night
To mortal men, he, with his horrid crew,
Lay vanquished, rolling in the fiery gulf,
Confounded, though immortal. But his doom
Reserved him to more wrath; for now the thought
Both of lost happiness and lasting pain
Torments him: round he throws his baleful eyes,
That witnessed huge affliction and dismay,

---

33. Sure, blame the snake. Obviously our ability to blame our parents or others for our own problems goes back much farther than Freud. Heck, the snake didn't give Eve the apple; he doesn't even have arms for corn's sake.

Mixed with obdurate pride and steadfast hate.
At once, as far as Angels ken, he views
The dismal situation waste and wild.
A dungeon horrible, on all sides round,
As one great furnace flamed; yet from those flames
No light; but rather darkness visible
Served only to discover sights of woe,
Regions of sorrow, doleful shades, where peace
And rest can never dwell, hope never comes
That comes to all, but torture without end
Still urges, and a fiery deluge, fed
With ever-burning sulphur unconsumed.
Such place eternal justice has prepared
For those rebellious;[34] here their prison ordained
In utter darkness, and their portion set,
As far removed from God and light of Heaven
As from the centre thrice to the utmost pole.
Oh how unlike the place from whence they fell!
There the companions of his fall, o'erwhelmed
With floods and whirlwinds of tempestuous fire,
He soon discerns; and, weltering by his side,
One next himself in power, and next in crime,
Long after known in Palestine, and named
Beelzebub. To whom the Arch-Enemy,
And thence in heaven called Satan, with bold words
Breaking the horrid silence, thus began:—
"If thou beest he—but O how fallen! how changed
From him who, in the happy realms of light
Clothed   with   transcendent   brightness,   didst
outshine
Myriads, though bright!—if he whom mutual league,
United thoughts and counsels, equal hope

---

34. So eat your peas boys and girls. Fiery rain, heat, smells—keep it up and you'll go to New Orleans in August.

And hazard in the glorious enterprise
Joined with me once, now misery hath joined
In equal ruin; into what pit thou seest
From what height fallen: so much the stronger
proved
He with his thunder; and till then who knew
The force of those dire arms? Yet not for those,
Nor what the potent Victor in his rage
Can else inflict, do I repent, or change,
Though changed in outward lustre, that fixed mind,
And high disdain from sense of injured merit,
That with the mightiest raised me to contend,
And to the fierce contentions brought along
Innumerable force of spirits armed,
That durst dislike his reign, and, me preferring,
His utmost power with adverse power opposed
In dubious battle on the plains of Heaven,
And shook his throne. What though the field be
lost?
All is not lost—the unconquerable will,
And study of revenge, immortal hate,
And courage never to submit or yield:
And what is else not to be overcome?
That glory never shall his wrath or might
Extort from me. To bow and sue for grace
With suppliant knee, and deify his power
Who, from the terror of this arm, so late
Doubted his empire—that were low indeed;
That were an ignominy and shame beneath
This downfall; since, by fate, the strength of Gods,
And this empyreal substance, cannot fail;
Since, through experience of this great event,
In arms not worse, in foresight much advanced,
We may with more successful hope resolve
To wage by force or guile eternal war,

Irreconcilable to our grand foe,
Who now triumphs, and in the excess of joy
Sole reigning holds the tyranny of heaven."
So spake the apostate angel, though in pain,
Vaunting aloud, but racked with deep despair;
And him thus answered soon his bold compeer:—
"O Prince, O Chief of many throned powers
That led the embattled Seraphim to war
Under thy conduct, and, in dreadful deeds
Fearless, endangered heaven's perpetual king,
And put to proof his high supremacy,
Whether upheld by strength, or chance, or fate,
Too well I see and rue the dire event
That, with sad overthrow and foul defeat,
Hath lost us heaven, and all this mighty host
In horrible destruction laid thus low,
As far as Gods and heavenly essences
Can perish: for the mind and spirit remains
Invincible, and vigour soon returns,
Though all our glory extinct, and happy state
Here swallowed up in endless misery.

And so it goes forever and ever. Maybe it was just Milton's way of showing us what eternity really feels like, but I somehow doubt it. Is *Paradise Lost* a great work? Absolutely. But I kind of wish someone had grabbed John by the lapels and said, "ENOUGH ALREADY!"

EIGHT

Liberal Guilt and Ripping Yarns

Robinson Crusoe

> September 30, 1659. I, poor miserable Robinson
> Crusoe, being shipwrecked during a dreadful storm in
> the offing, came on shore on this dismal, unfortunate
> island, which I called "the Island of Despair," all the
> rest of the ship's company being drowned and myself
> almost dead...

At last, a novel. Something I can get my teeth into. *Robinson Crusoe* by Daniel Defoe is one of those books everyone knows about, and I can't believe I have never read it. I've read *Moll Flanders* and *The Book of Pyrates*, so unlike any of the other writers I've encountered so far, I had a very good idea of what I was up against.

Everyone knows the story, or at least thinks they do. I discovered several things as I read the book though:

1. He was marooned in the Caribbean, not the South Seas.
2. The famous footprint he found in the sand was there eight years before he ever met Friday—the footprint belonged to someone else.
3. He was on the island for twenty-seven years.
4. The book actually ends in a snowy mountain pass

between Spain and France.

5. After the huge success of *Robinson Crusoe*, there were actually two sequels, both failed miserably. There is no truth to the rumor that one was called The Phantom Menace.

It's impossible at the distance of all these years to judge what an outrageous success this book must have been at the time it came out. There had been very few novels written to this point, and most were a retelling of stories that had been around for years, stories like *Robin Hood* and *King Arthur*.

This one was doubly refreshing because it was based loosely on a true story. Telling outright lies about true events is a tradition as old as man, but to do it and let everyone know it's a fabrication was almost unheard of.

The story is based on the life of Alexander Selkirk, who was shipwrecked off the coast of Chile and survived on a deserted island until he was rescued only a few years before Defoe's book came out. Everyone in Europe had heard his story and Defoe was not above seeing there was a buck to be made in hitching himself to the phenomenon.

It was an immediate smash, and it really set the benchmark for the adventure novel for the next 200 years. His story influenced everything from fiction writers like Robert L. Stevenson, who modeled the marooned pirate Ben Gunn on Crusoe, to real-life adventurers like Burton[35] and Shackleton whose boyhood fantasies of adventure and travel were stoked by the story.

It's easy to see how this book was so popular for so long. It has shipwrecks, bloodthirsty savages, near misses and the obligatory minority sidekick. In fact, I'm pretty sure Defoe takes credit for the long line of sidekicks who get no credit, assume the subservient role and

---

35. Sir Richard Francis Burton. I unabashedly put him on the list of historical people I'd want to have dinner with. How can anyone not dig a champion swordsman, master of forty languages, Sufi mystic, and world-class pornographer.

regularly pull the white guy's bacon out of the fire. This line includes Tonto (Apache) Kato (Asian of some description) and Murtaugh in the Lethal Weapon movies (right, you bought the ticket because you've been pining for the next Danny Glover movie).

It was a smash from its first publication until the invention of movies. Benjamin Franklin loved the book. So did Churchill. Generations of white guys learned how the universe works from books just like this. The world was a place to be conquered, the white guy's ingenuity will always keep him alive and ultimately he'll subdue the savages. What's not to like?

Which brings us to why I also completely get why the book has fallen out of favor: It has two strikes against it right away, race and religion. Let's face it, with the exception of Adam Sandler's appeal there are few things more divisive in the world today.

Now here's the question before the court: At what point does the racial, religious or other beliefs of an author disqualify a work from the pantheon?

Think about it, Defoe actually had a pretty good run—his book was a best-seller for 200 years. Wagner only lasted about forty before Hitler adopted him and pretty much got him banned from the canon until recently. Lest you think I'm overstating the negative effects of a connection with Hitler, let me ask you a question: How many kids named Adolph do you know?

DW Griffiths was a pretty good little filmmaker but one little lapse of judgment—assuming you can call making the Klu Klux Klan the heroes of a film a little anything—has him reduced to "oh-yeah-him-too" status when you talk about great directors.

The racial issue in Robinson Crusoe is a huge hulking elephant in the room. What bothered me is not the blatant things that usually draw attention to (like his paternalistic attitude to Friday); it's the casual references and assumptions that the audience agrees with Crusoe's thinking. Worse, to my tender sensibilities, Defoe was probably right about that.

As a time capsule of how people in that era thought, it's fabulous. As something you want your kids to read and admire, it's far from a white guy's proudest moment.

I will admit that my first reaction when I hear people scream about racism in books, especially old books, is "get over yourself." I would like to think that people are capable of reading something and making intelligent decisions about what is acceptable and not. After all, that's how people thought in the seventeenth century; it makes sense that a book written then would contain that attitude. It doesn't mean we have to believe it's still acceptable.

Of course I would also like to think that people love their children, always act in their own best interest, and understand the issues before they vote. You see my dilemma. It's worse when you realize that for most of the last 100 years, Crusoe was read by young boys, whose discernment is suspect at best. I try to imagine any young kid in our schools today of whatever color or background reading this book and I'm suddenly not so protective of it. First amendment be damned.

So why is this book different than something like *Huckleberry Finn*? On the surface, it's far less offensive; after all, the "n" word is never spoken. Finn though was intended as satire, and it's an American book covering a vital era in American history. Crusoe was never intended to be anything other than entertainment. Tie goes to the book with serious intent.

Objectionable words aside, there's more than enough in Crusoe to make an enlightened human squirm.

Let's start with the fact that our boy Rob gets shipwrecked on a trip to Africa to buy slaves. No guilt, no moral dilemma, not even the decency of a Jefferson to at least question the institution. Nope, there's land to be worked and a buck to be made. Sign me up.

The ultimate proof that he never gave a thought to the slavery is that when, in the pits of despair, he wonders why God would punish him so severely, the reason he comes up with is that he disobeyed his father and ran off to sea. The fact that he was planning to buy, sell, and enslave other human beings didn't even make the top ten list.

It's not that he hates Africans, you understand. He simply hasn't given the matter much thought. He assumes his superiority over everyone else in the book, including (especially?) Friday.

To be fair, Friday volunteers to be his servant after Crusoe rescues him from cannibals, but never for a moment does our boy question the order of things. His "man" is a better shot than he is, saves his life three times including in a snow-filled mountain pass with 300 wolves and a ravenous bear. Crusoe only takes this as the natural order of things.

This thinking still survives in the minds of many middle managers, by the way.

But what about all those generations of people who read the book? What message did they take away? The message was never explicit—hat this is how it should be—it was implicit: This is how it is.

In an age when most people, especially in Colonial Britain, never actually met someone from another country—never mind a different race or culture—these images formed the opinions of millions of people. These images and characters were the closest most people would come to a Friday, or a Pocahontas or an Uncas, and so was shaped a worldview. Foreigners were ignorant, passive, and grateful to the white man. Darned right we run the place.

I thought about if I were African American, or Native American. Hell I'm a Canadian American and it makes me squirm in my chair worse than when I watched *Grease 2* with my eight-year-old.

So maybe the book is no longer an appropriate book for kids. Maybe it takes a level of maturity and discernment most readers don't have to take Crusoe's beliefs at face value and accept them in the context of time and place: to simply enjoy the story.

While the issue of race is the big complaint about Crusoe, and the reason usually given for its decline in popularity, I wonder about another reason. I was completely unaware of how big a part religion played in the book.

In the beginning of the book, Crusoe is a rebellious teenager, certainly not given to lofty thoughts.

After he's shipwrecked, however, he finds a bible among some things that wash ashore. In his solitude, and driven more by boredom than search for solace, he begins to read it. At first, he only appreciates his physical salvation, glad he got out alive and curious why God spared him. Later, he develops a deeper faith, going so far as to keep the Sabbath. On one level, I can admire that. On the other hand, since there's no football or white sales, what's he giving up? It's a deserted island for crying out loud!

There's a mature spirituality at work here, especially for a layman of Defoe's time. He ponders the souls of the cannibals and comes to the conclusion that since they don't know about Christ, they probably aren't doomed to hell and their actions make a kind of sense. Pretty advanced for an Englishman in the 1650s. I had a seventh-grade Sunday school teacher who hadn't worked that one out by 1970. He has a real concern for the soul of Friday and most others he meets.

He even sells his ranch in Brazil[36] rather than live in a Catholic country and face the wrath of the Inquisition, which was still active in Spanish and Portuguese colonies.

His spiritual journey is all very matter-of-fact. No irony, no dramatic renunciation of traditional values; in fact, quite the opposite. He becomes much more spiritual as a result of his trials. I wonder how that would play today.

Can you imagine a popular book or movie where the main character actually embraces religion at the end of the story? I mean, it's not that farfetched to think that if I were washed up on a desert island for twenty-seven years I would probably give some thought to my immortal soul.

---

36. This guy spends twenty-seven years on a desert island and he owns a ranch. I can't get a house and as spotty as my employment record is, it doesn't have that kind of a gap in my resume!

I can't imagine it. In the movie *Castaway*, the most intense discussion Tom Hanks has is with a volleyball in what I can only assume is an attempt to get in touch with his inner air bladder.

Anything smacking of religion, Christianity in particular, is relegated to the ghetto of Christian literature; a shadowy place populated by chaste romance novels and the *Left Behind* series. For the uninitiated this is a series of novels based on a literal interpretation of the book of Revelations, a thought that makes me pine for the rock-solid realism of Hinduism.[37]

Some 250 years after it was written I'm struck by the simple declarations of faith. I know it's a feel-good ending designed to be instructive to the masses and all that, but it doesn't feel preachy or self-righteous like *Pilgrim's Progress,* one of the classics of seventeenth century English Lit, which has all the subtlety and style of a crowbar to the cranium.

Robinson Crusoe went through a traumatic experience and came out a changed man, probably a better one. For a lot of reasons the book might deserve to be forgotten or at least ignored. For a few good ones I'm going to remember it for a long time.

I chose the chapter of *Robinson Crusoe* where we meet Friday. I did this for two reasons:

1. you can judge Defoe's attitude towards non-whites for yourself and;
2. you can win a bar bet. Friday wasn't black—he was a Carib Indian (not that I'm sure Defoe knew the difference).

Also, I am warning you now: Do not attempt to read this aloud. There is one paragraph—heck a sentence—that goes for a page and a half. You could hurt yourself....

---

37. If you can tell me a quantitative difference between an elephant-headed, eight-armed goddess and a seven-horned dragon, you're a better man than I am, Gunga Din.

ROBINSON CRUSOE
— Daniel Defoe, 1719

Chapter 6

I was surpriz'd one morning early, with seeing no less than five *Canoes* all on shore together on my side of the island; and the people who belong'd to them all landed, and out of my sight: The number of them broke all my measures, for seeing so many, and knowing that they always came four or six, or sometimes more in a boat, I could not tell what to think of it, or how to take my measures, to attack twenty or thirty men single-handed; so I lay still in my castle, perplex'd and discomforted: however I put my self into all the same postures for an attack that I had formerly provided, and was just ready for action, if anything had presented; having waited a good while, listening to hear if they made any noise; at length being very impatient, I set my guns at the foot of my ladder, and clamber'd up to the top of the hill, by my two stages as usual; standing so however that my head did not appear above the hill, so that they could not perceive me by any means; here I observ'd by the help of my perspective glass, that they were no less than thirty in number, that they had a fire kindled, that they had had meat dress'd. How they had cook'd it, that I knew not, or what it was; but they were all dancing in I know not how many barbarous gestures and figures, their own way, round the fire.

While I was thus looking on them, I perceived by my perspective, two miserable wretches dragg'd from the boats, where it seems they were laid by, and were now brought out for the slaughter. I perceived one of them immediately fell, being knock'd down, I suppose with a club or wooden sword, for that was their way, and two or three others were at work immediately cutting him open for their cookery, while the other victim was left standing by himself, till they should be ready for him. In that very moment this poor wretch seeing himself a little at liberty, Nature inspir'd him with hopes of life, and he started away from them, and ran with incredible swiftness along the sands directly towards me, I mean towards that part of the coast, where my habitation was.

I was dreadfully frighted, (that I must acknowledge) when I perceived him to run my way; and especially, when as I thought I saw him pursued by the whole body, and now I expected that part of my dream was coming to pass, and that he would certainly take shelter in my grove; but I could not depend by any means upon my dream for the rest of it, (viz.) that the other savages would not pursue him thither, and find him there. However I kept my station, and my spirits began to recover, when I found that there was not above three Men that follow'd him, and still more was I encourag'd, when I found that he outstrip'd them exceedingly in running, and gain'd ground of them, so that if he could but hold it for half an hour, I saw easily he would fairly get away from them all.

There was between them and my castle, the creek which I mention'd often at the first part of my story, when I landed my cargoes out of the ship; and this I saw plainly, he must necessarily swim over, or the poor wretch would be taken there: But when the Savage escaping came thither, he made nothing of it, tho' the tide was then up, but plunging in, swam thro' in about thirty strokes or thereabouts, landed and ran on with exceeding strength and swiftness; when the three persons came to the Creek, I found that two of them could swim, but the third cou'd not, and that standing on the other side, he look'd at the other, but went no further; and soon after went softly back again, which as it happen'd, was very well for him in the main.

I observ'd, that the two who swam, were yet more than twice as long swimming over the Creek, as the fellow was, that fled from them: It came now very warmly upon my thoughts, and indeed irresistibly, that now was my time to get me a Servant,[38] and perhaps a companion, or assistant; and that I was call'd

---

38. Okay, the guy's racing for his life and all Robinson can think of is, "Boy, I'll bet he can fetch me a beer in no time flat—NOW he's worth saving". Still, it's a pretty good adventure story.

plainly by Providence to save this poor creature's life; I
immediately run down the ladders with all possible expedition,
fetches my two guns, for they were both but at the foot of the
ladders, as I observ'd above; and getting up again, with the same
haste, to the top of the hill, I cross'd toward the sea; and having
a very short cut, and all down hill, clapp'd my self in the way,
between the pursuers, and the pursu'd; hallowing aloud to him
that fled, who looking back, was at first perhaps as much
frighted at me, as at them; but I beckon'd with my hand to him,
to come back; and in the mean time, I slowly advanc'd towards
the two that follow'd; then rushing at once upon the foremost, I
knock'd him down with the stock of my piece I was loath to fire,
because I would not have the rest hear; though at that distance,
it would not have been easily heard, and being out of sight of the
smoke too, they wou'd not have easily known what to make of it:
having knock'd this fellow down, the other who pursu'd with him
stopp'd, as if he had been frighted; and I advanc'd a-pace
towards him; but as I came nearer, I perceiv'd presently, he had a
bow and arrow, and was fitting it to shoot at me; so I was then
necessitated to shoot at him first, which I did, and kill'd him at
the first shoot; the poor savage who fled, but had stopp'd;
though he saw both his enemies fallen, and kill'd, as he thought;
yet was so frighted with the fire, and noise of my piece, that he
stood stock still, and neither came forward or went backward,
tho' he seem'd rather enclin'd to fly still, than to come on.

I hollow'd again to him, and made signs to come forward,
which he easily understood, and came a little way, then stopp'd
again, and then a little further, and stopp'd again, and I cou'd
then perceive that he stood trembling, as if he had been taken
Prisoner, and had just been to be kill'd, as his two enemies were;
I beckon'd him again to come to me, and gave him all the signs
of encouragement that I could think of, and he came nearer and
nearer, kneeling down every ten or twelve steps in token of
acknowledgement for my saving his Life: I smil'd at him, and
look'd pleasantly, and beckon'd to him to come still nearer; at
length he came close to me, and then he kneel'd down again,

kiss'd the ground, and laid his head upon the ground, and taking me by the foot, set my foot upon his head; this it seems was in token of swearing to be my slave for ever; I took him up, and made much of him, and encourag'd him all I could.[39]

But there was more work to do yet, for I perceived the savage who I knock'd down, was not kill'd, but stunn'd with the blow, and began to come to himself; so I pointed to him, and showing him the savage, that he was not dead; upon this he spoke some words to me, and though I could not understand them, yet I thought they were pleasant to hear, for they were the first sound of a man's voice, that I had heard, *my own excepted*, for above twenty five years.

But there was no time for such reflections now, the savage who was knock'd down recover'd himself so far, as to sit up upon the ground, and I perceived that my savage began to be afraid; but when I saw that, I presented my other piece at the man, as if I would shoot him, upon this my Savage, *for so I call him now*, made a motion to me to lend him my sword, which hung naked in a belt by my side; so I did: he no sooner had it, but he runs to his enemy, and at one blow cut off his head as cleaverly, no executioner in *Germany*, could have done it sooner or better; which I thought very strange, for one who I had reason to believe never saw a sword in his life before, except their own wooden swords; however it seems, as I learn'd afterwards, they make their wooden swords so sharp, so heavy, and the wood is so hard, that they will cut off heads even with them, ay and arms, and that at one blow too; when he had done this, he comes laughing to me in sign of triumph, and brought me the sword again, and with abundance of gestures which I did not understand, laid it down with the head of the savage, that he'd kill'd just before me....

---

39. Yeah, if someone wanted to be my slave for life I'd encourage them too. Does HR know about this hiring policy? Of course it's not much more arcane than the Meyers Briggs.

NINE

California Dreamin'

Stories by Bret Harte

> The effect of the poem on Sierra Flat was remarkable and unprecedented. The absolute vileness of its doggerel, the gratuitous imbecility of its thought, and above all the crowning audacity of the fact that it was the work of a citizen and published in the county paper, brought it instantly into popularity.
>
> — Bret Harte, "The Poet of Sierra Flat"

Short stories. Now we're getting somewhere. Of all the types of writing out there, this is the one that I have enjoyed the most. Not coincidentally, it's the one that I've done the most of myself, with absolutely no success (he adds bitterly), but that doesn't stop me from considering myself a short story writer and therefore not intimidated by the form.

It's not like poetry, which I haven't had much experience with, or a novel, that always struck me as an unattainable goal. I mean what real human being is going to write a 400-page novel? Thirteen pages in a short story, now there's something a guy like me, meaning someone with limited talent and an even shorter attention span, can handle.

From Poe to Kipling to Tolstoy to Cheever, I thought I knew most of the writers who might qualify as "classic," but who the #$%^ is Bret Harte when he's home? I'm guessing it's not the same guy who left daddy's wrestling circuit in Calgary to become a wrestler named, The Hit Man, but who knows?

Turns out he's a writer of short stories who burned bright for a while and stayed around long past the time his best work was done, which is good for the writer personally, I suppose, but hard on his posterity. Longevity is sometimes a very bad career move.

His area of expertise was the California gold rush. As a teacher in the mining camps and then a newspaper writer in San Francisco, he had a front row seat to the events that created California and became a very big star in the process. He became well known for his comic stories of life in the mining camps, got rich and promptly left San Francisco for the real cultural centers of New York, Boston and London, wanting to write about really important things and people that mattered.

Sadly for Harte, he never wrote anything else that was worth a damn.

Once he tackled a topic other than California, the muse deserted him. He lived thirty years past the time his best stories were written, eventually winding up as a minor diplomat in Germany and Scotland and living off his reputation.

So how did he wind up in this august collection? On my bookshelf he sits between Benjamin Franklin and Homer, which I'm sure he'd appreciate (apparently our boy Bret was a man of prodigious ego). At first blush, the doings in Poker Flat or Logport Bay don't have much in common with the great minds of Athens or London. A more cynical brain than mine might guess that it was because his work was in public domain and it was an inexpensive way to fill a slow month. And nobody expected the middle-class poseurs who bought these books to actually read them.

On the other hand, the purpose of Classics Club was to introduce readers to writers they otherwise never would have discovered, and I think it's safe to say I'd have never come across his stuff any other way.

So anyway, this East Coast dandified schoolteacher finds himself in the mining camps. This is a whole new world for him: people who have completely deserted their families and everything they've known to chase fame and fortune. People from all over the world with different faces and indecipherable accents—exotic places like Paris, Kowloon, and Texas—gathered together to form communities with no observable bond other than the quest for riches.

Having lived in California for almost ten years, I can tell you that nothing's changed. Whether it's gold in the 1850s (odds of success were microscopic; they had to cut all ties to their past and most of them died broke or crazy) or the movie and TV business to this very minute (odds of success are microscopic; cut all ties to your past, most of them will die broke or crazy) California has always been the home office of those willing to roll the dice.

Think about it. California was not even a blip on the radar screen until gold was discovered. The Spanish considered it a waste of energy, everyone knew Mexico was the land of riches. California is where they sent the screw-ups and the otter hunters.

Gradually though, starting with the Gold Rush and continuing till today, it filled up with people doing what Americans have always done when their feet itched or their older brothers inherited the farm and all the money—moved west.

What's happened to California isn't that it's such a paradise that people can't leave; it's just they can't go any further west without learning Japanese, so there they sit. Thirty-two million people who didn't care much for their own families and friends now have to find a way to get along. Not only that, now we're into fourth and fifth generation Californians, and it's not getting much better. While some have real roots and a sense of family, most are just plain genetically programmed for detachment. Homesickness is a recessive gene.

I compare that to my little western suburb of Chicago. After only a year I can name almost all my neighbors, or at least their kids and dogs.

They all know each other intimately because they've been here for years; many went to high school together.

Not only have they been in the same house for multiple years (a concept the gypsy in me can barely grasp) but many are wracked with guilt because they had to leave the "old neighborhood," usually somewhere on the south side, to move so far away from their folks. Far in the Midwest apparently is defined being in the next area code.

So the Midwest is made up of people to whom family and place are so important nothing—and if a Chicago winter doesn't motivate you to get the heck out nothing will—can make them leave. California, on the other hand, is comprised primarily of people who were either the black sheep of their families or were so driven by the need to succeed in a way they never would had they stuck it out in Des Moines, or Buffalo[40] or wherever.

So, you have an entire population of nomads with nowhere to roam. Not exactly a recipe for peace in our time. You also have the not-particularly-pretty fact that California is, if nothing else, the world's most spectacularly successful real estate scam.

Don't look at me like that, it's true. Yes, the weather is very hard to beat and there are precious few bugs, but the entire image and economy of Southern California is built on a big greasy lie designed to sell real estate.

You know those palm trees that look so good on TV? Transplants. They don't grow there naturally.

The beautiful lawns and flowers you see in the gardens? Transplants. They don't grow there naturally.

The beautiful women you see in music videos? Well, those are *implants*, but the point is they don't grow there naturally.

Anyone who has visited Southern California will attest to the fact

---

40. It's only in thinking about this issue of home and place that Buffalo, NY makes any sense to me at all. After having performed there for years, I wanted to say to folks "You know, there's no fence around this city, why don't you just go?" Yet they stay and claim to love it, mysterious as that is. I firmly believe the reason it snows so much there is because even God doesn't want to look at that town and tries to bury it three months of the year.

that the beautiful green you see only exists naturally about two months of the year usually around January so that they can mock the rest of the country on New Year's Day. The rest of the time it's a desert.

Lawns wouldn't exist, palm trees wouldn't grow and the San Fernando Valley would be nothing but jackrabbits and porno studios if it weren't for water piped in from elsewhere. Yup, even the water is transplanted.

I also alluded to the fact that it was a particularly successful scam. Here's my best argument on this one: California is the only place in the world where the natural disasters affect the rich people.

You hear about some mud slide in Bangladesh that wipes out thousands of people or an earthquake that destroys a village in Guatemala and you can be sure it's because those people couldn't afford to live anywhere else. You hear about a mudslide in Malibu or an earthquake in San Francisco and it's million dollar condos that are involved. Not only do the rich in California live in the most dangerous area, they pay premiums to do so.

You can't move to a place where for thousands of years the ecology was built on two sure things:

1. the desert plants will probably be wiped out by fire every seven years or so;.

2. the mountains that look so pretty are in fact, overgrown sand dunes prone to mudslides, and by the way, probably won't be where they are now in a few years because Mother Nature keeps rearranging the furniture.

Given these facts, what kind of knucklehead builds a house on stilts on a hillside, gets rid of the ground cover that keeps the hillside in place but leaves the big trees that reach right next to his roof, then wonders why he can't get insurance? It's like these guys figure, "I have enough money, God won't #$%^ with me."

It's no coincidence by the way that the two most profitable businesses in Southern California are real estate and pornography. Real estate agents survive by selling arid land that is inherently unstable and ripe for disaster, but they can always find a buyer. Pornographers sell *people* that are inherently unstable and ripe for disaster, but you can always find a buyer.

I'm no smarter, by the way. Immediately after the 1994 Northridge quake wiped out every piece of glassware in our Reseda house, we replaced it and promptly moved—to Northridge. I suppose it was some kind of Lightning Doesn't Strike Twice theory but thinking back on it now I needed a big slap to the melon. Apparently, I'd been in California long enough.

Still, the Eagles weren't far wrong when, in talking about the Hotel California they said, "You can check out any time you like, but you can never leave." With everything that's wrong with California—a list I can give you alphabetically or by geography—it was hard to leave because of the weather, especially for this humble Canadian lad.

The Duchess grew up in Miami Beach and lived in L.A for twenty-eight years. Her Serene Highness was born in Glendale, she has never known winter except as something on TV and Christmas cards, and aware vaguely that it was to be dreaded. I, on the other hand, am Canadian and knew exactly what I was getting us into.

If I live long enough, The Duchess might someday forgive me. I have no such hope for my daughter, who has already informed me I've ruined her life and she can't wait to go to college in California.

I suspect this is some kind of revenge for the one piece of cruelty I have knowingly committed (repeatedly I might add) against my fellow man. I used to get no greater thrill than calling friends in Toronto on Christmas Eve (Toronto being so much more miserable in the winter than Vancouver and thus more ripe for the abuse), apologizing for not calling them earlier in the day, but I'd been in the back yard picking oranges. The fact that it was true made it no less evil, and I'm guessing there's a special corner of hell reserved for me. Their screams of anguish made it almost worth the price my Karma will pay, *hehehehhehehe.*

I can't imagine how exotic California must have seemed to Bret Harte when he first arrived, nor what San Francisco looked like at the time, with its mixture of faces from just about everywhere *but* Connecticut. It obviously impressed him though, because it broke some kind of creative dam for him, stories and poetry flooding out.

Most are pretty darned good, if not anything I haven't seen elsewhere. It's a lot like Mark Twain's stuff without the jumping frog, and the poetry is just like Robert Service, the stuff that every Canadian kid got force fed because at least "The Cremation of Sam McGee" was reasonably funny, and dead bodies can keep almost anyone fascinated for the length of one English Lit class.

As I read through them, one thought kept occurring to me: There are very few women. When Harte writes about a woman it's usually a love story where the one woman in the camp has her pick of men, finds one (usually setting off some kind of alpha male brouhaha in the process) and then leaves the camp, even more estrogen-deprived than it was earlier.

That's pretty much my idea of hell—a place where there are no women. For one thing, there's the whole issue of sex or its alternatives. All those men just stewing in their own testosterone with no outlet. There's a toxic substance I wouldn't bury in Yucca Mountain.

It's not just sex, although if I were living in any place where the men outnumbered the women by 17 to 1, I am afraid I know where I'd be on that pecking order (about number 14, unless Stumpy's goiter got removed and then I'm number 15 with a bullet) and I know how cranky I'd be about it. No wonder there was such a high murder rate in the camps—booze and unlaid miners just can't be good for the common weal.

Emerson said, "The unexamined life is not worth living," to which I'm tempted to add, "Neither is one without women in it."

Chicks.

Broads.

Skirts.

Dames.

I love'em all, even the ones I can't stand. They make the world smell good. They civilize us and inspire us. Harte knew the impact one good woman could have on a bunch of men. Whether it's the saving angel of "Miggles" or Miss Mary the schoolmarm in "The Idyl of Red Gulch," or the almost feral Mliss, women are the "other" that makes men want to be better than they are.

They're our moms for crying out loud, a fact for which I'm eternally grateful. If childbearing were left up to the men of the planet, overpopulation would not be on the top ten problems list.

Living in an all-male environment like a mining camp, prison, or fraternity house is as awful a fate as I can imagine. I can't imagine being gay. It's not that the gory details are repulsive; I'm just not crazy about men. My hat is sincerely off to gay couples who want to wed because I can't imagine a seriously monogamous relationship with two men in the equation. It's hard enough with one!

I can't imagine ever being horny enough to be turned on by, well, by me. Yes, a few select women in the world have been (and every second Saturday at least one still is, God bless her) and if that ain't reason enough to worship the ground their twenty-three pairs of shoes trod upon, I don't know what is.

It is one of the weird things about my life that I just plain like women better than men. Always have. I don't recall ever going through one of those "girls have cooties" stages. I always wanted to hang with them. Of course, few girls ever mastered either the noogie or the wedgie, and as both a chronic nerd and a runt I knew where I was better off.

To this day, if I think about the friends I really treasure—the ones who know my darkest secrets and still talk to me—they are almost exclusively women. Whether it's the Jewish bellydancer cum performance artist or the bisexual customs guard/attorney who was the first girl I ever knew with real boobs, I adore them deeply, and if you put a gun to my head[41] to choose someone in my life, they would be at the top of the list. Yes, The Duchess is my best friend, but wives don't count. I've had two of them, I know.

Now this is not to imply that I have handed in my cajones. It's not like I'm some kind of platonic saint. I have sexual feelings towards not only these women but most women walking the earth, it's just that when the trade-off came between having them in my life and having sex with them, (or more to the point, pushing for sex to the point where it became whining and not a little embarrassing) I opted to have them as friends. Proving once again I occasionally exercise good judgment. Well, good judgment and total fear of a sexual harassment suit if any of the women I work with knew what really goes on in my fevered mind.

So Harte's stories do what good stories are supposed to do, paint the picture of a time and place I can't imagine myself in otherwise.

What is it like to be in a place full of desperate, rootless men, devoid of female influence or companionship, built on a mirage of instant wealth? His stories tell us. If nothing else, it saves me a trip to Vegas with the boys.

This story is one I think sums up everything that is good about Harte's stories. It's just the first part, but it gives a pretty good idea of the tone of moral superiority mixed with actual affection. Kind of like Marlin Perkins used to exhibit when he sat in the tent and made tea while Jim went out to wrestle the gators.

THE LUCK OF ROARING CAMP
— Bret Harte, 1867

There was commotion in Roaring Camp. It could not have been a fight, for in 1850 that was not novel enough to have called together the entire settlement. The ditches and claims

---

41. And just to prove my point, only a man would do such a thing. Women could nag it out of you much quicker and more precisely.

were not only deserted, but "Tuttle's Grocery" had contributed its gamblers, who, it will be remembered, calmly continued their game the day that French Pete and Kanaka Joe shot each other to death over the bar in the front room.

The whole camp was collected before a rude cabin on the outer edge of the clearing. Conversation was carried on in a low tone, but the name of a woman was frequently repeated. It was a name familiar enough in the camp,—"Cherokee Sal."

Perhaps the less said of her the better. She was a coarse and, it is to be feared, a very sinful woman. But at that time she was the only woman in Roaring Camp, and was just then lying in sore extremity, when she most needed the ministration of her own sex.

Dissolute, abandoned, and irreclaimable, she was yet suffering a martyrdom hard enough to bear even when veiled by sympathizing womanhood, but now terrible in her loneliness.

The primal curse had come to her in that original isolation which must have made the punishment of the first transgression so dreadful. It was, perhaps, part of the expiation of her sin that, at a moment when she most lacked her sex's intuitive tenderness and care, she met only the half-contemptuous faces of her masculine associates.

Yet a few of the spectators were, I think, touched by her sufferings. Sandy Tipton thought it was "rough on Sal," and, in the contemplation of her condition, for a moment rose superior to the fact that he had an ace and two bowers in his sleeve.

It will be seen also that the situation was novel. Deaths were by no means uncommon in Roaring Camp, but a birth was a new thing. People had been dismissed the camp effectively, finally, and with no possibility of return; but this was the first time that anybody had been introduced AB INITIO.[42] Hence the excitement.

"You go in there, Stumpy," said a prominent citizen known as

---

42. Not surprisingly, Harte is exactly the kind of guy who would say AB INITIO and put it in capitals. This is why he lasted mere months as a school teacher in the camps before scurrying back to San Francisco.

"Kentuck," addressing one of the loungers. "Go in there, and see what you kin do. You've had experience in them things."

Perhaps there was a fitness in the selection. Stumpy, in other climes, had been the putative head of two families; in fact, it was owing to some legal informality in these proceedings that Roaring Camp—a city of refuge—was indebted to his company. The crowd approved the choice, and Stumpy was wise enough to bow to the majority. The door closed on the extempore surgeon and midwife, and Roaring Camp sat down outside, smoked its pipe, and awaited the issue.

The assemblage numbered about a hundred men. One or two of these were actual fugitives from justice, some were criminal, and all were reckless. Physically they exhibited no indication of their past lives and character. The greatest scamp had a Raphael face, with a profusion of blonde hair; Oakhurst, a gambler, had the melancholy air and intellectual abstraction of a Hamlet; the coolest and most courageous man was scarcely over five feet in height, with a soft voice and an embarrassed, timid manner.

The term "roughs" applied to them was a distinction rather than a definition. Perhaps in the minor details of fingers, toes, ears, etc., the camp may have been deficient, but these slight omissions did not detract from their aggregate force. The strongest man had but three fingers on his right hand; the best shot had but one eye.

Such was the physical aspect of the men that were dispersed around the cabin. The camp lay in a triangular valley between two hills and a river. The only outlet was a steep trail over the summit of a hill that faced the cabin, now illuminated by the rising moon The suffering woman might have seen it from the rude bunk whereon she lay,—seen it winding like a silver thread until it was lost in the stars above.

A fire of withered pine boughs added sociability to the gathering. By degrees the natural levity of Roaring Camp returned. Bets were freely offered and taken regarding the result. Three to five that "Sal would get through with it;" even that the child would survive; side bets as to the sex and complexion of the coming stranger.

In the midst of an excited discussion an exclamation came from those nearest the door, and the camp stopped to listen. Above the swaying and moaning of the pines, the swift rush of the river, and the crackling of the fire rose a sharp, querulous cry,—a cry unlike anything heard before in the camp. The pines stopped moaning, the river ceased to rush, and the fire to crackle. It seemed as if Nature had stopped to listen too.

The camp rose to its feet as one man! It was proposed to explode a barrel of gunpowder;[43] but in consideration of the situation of the mother, better counsels prevailed, and only a few revolvers were discharged; for whether owing to the rude surgery of the camp, or some other reason, Cherokee Sal was sinking fast.

Within an hour she had climbed, as it were, that rugged road that led to the stars, and so passed out of Roaring Camp, its sin and shame, forever. I do not think that the announcement disturbed them much, except in speculation as to the fate of the child. "Can he live now?" was asked of Stumpy. The answer was doubtful. The only other being of Cherokee Sal's sex and maternal condition in the settlement was an ass. There was some conjecture as to fitness, but the experiment was tried. It was less problematical than the ancient treatment of Romulus and Remus, and apparently as successful.

When these details were completed, which exhausted another hour, the door was opened, and the anxious crowd of men, who had already formed themselves into a queue, entered in single file. Beside the low bunk or shelf, on which the figure of the mother was starkly outlined below the blankets, stood a pine table. On this a candle-box was placed, and within it, swathed in staring red flannel, lay the last arrival at Roaring Camp. Beside the candle-box was placed a hat. Its use was soon indicated.

---

43. Again, male thinking. This is the same logic that had three supposedly wise men show up at a baby's birthday party with gold, frankincense, and myrrh. Not a diaper or a rattle in there anywhere. I despair for my own sex sometimes.

"Gentlemen," said Stumpy, with a singular mixture of authority and EX OFFICIO complacency,— "gentlemen will please pass in at the front door, round the table, and out at the back door. Them as wishes to contribute anything toward the orphan will find a hat handy."

The first man entered with his hat on; he uncovered, however, as he looked about him, and so unconsciously set an example to the next. In such communities good and bad actions are catching. As the procession filed in comments were audible,—criticisms addressed perhaps rather to Stumpy in the character of showman; "Is that him?"

"Mighty small specimen;" "Has n't more 'n got the color;" "Ain't bigger nor a derringer."

The contributions were as characteristic: A silver tobacco box; a doubloon; a navy revolver, silver mounted; a gold specimen; a very beautifully embroidered lady's handkerchief (from Oakhurst the gambler); a diamond breastpin; a diamond ring (suggested by the pin, with the remark from the giver that he "saw that pin and went two diamonds better"); a slung-shot; a Bible (contributor not detected); a golden spur; a silver teaspoon (the initials, I regret to say, were not the giver's); a pair of surgeon's shears; a lancet; a Bank of England note for 5 pounds; and about $200 in loose gold and silver coin.

During these proceedings Stumpy maintained a silence as impassive as the dead on his left, a gravity as inscrutable as that of the newly born on his right.

Only one incident occurred to break the monotony of the curious procession. As Kentuck bent over the candle-box half curiously, the child turned, and, in a spasm of pain, caught at his groping finger, and held it fast for a moment. Kentuck looked foolish and embarrassed. Something like a blush tried to assert itself in his weather-beaten cheek. "The damned little cuss!" he said, as he extricated his finger, with perhaps more tenderness and care than he might have been deemed capable of showing.

He held that finger a little apart from its fellows as he went out, and examined it curiously. The examination provoked the same original remark in regard to the child. In fact, he seemed to enjoy repeating it. "He rastled with my finger," he remarked to Tipton, holding up the member, "the damned little cuss!"

And so it goes. Not to spoil the story for you, but the tale doesn't end well. Read it your darn selves.

TEN

Good Government and Lousy Baby-Sitting

Essays of John Locke

> To understand political power aright, and derive it from its original, we must consider what estate all men are naturally in, and that is, a state of perfect freedom to order their actions, and dispose of their possessions and persons as they think fit, within the bounds of the laws of Nature, without asking leave or depending upon the will of any other man.
>
> —John Locke, "Second Treatise on Civil Government," 1690

What do you do with someone who is equal parts brilliant and full of hooey?

How much slack do you cut someone? When does their credibility take a hit sufficient to discount all the good stuff you find there?

Here's where context is so important, and why you can't divorce History and Literature, or Philosophy either for all that. I am a little afraid that this leads down a very windy postmodern garden path that says if it's all context, nothing is ever really true or of more value than anything else, and frankly, I don't know if I'm man enough to go there. Regardless, here we sit and if I'm going to get through this book of essays, time and place is of vital importance.

I do know that I haven't been able to read any of these books so far without taking into account what was going on at the time they were written. I can't believe how helpful the little essays before each volume have been. I'd have been completely at sea if I didn't have some idea of the political and social climate at the time they were written, if only to get the references.

Here's my advice for what it's worth: Don't read anything over 100 years old without reading the introductory essay first, and they all have introductory essays. In this case it's by Howard R. Penniman, whoever that is, and it reminded me of some things I really needed to know if I was going to have the foggiest notion what Locke was talking about, let alone have a sense of whether or not it was valid. For example:

1. He wrote during the Civil War in England
2. Very few laymen had written on religion, philosophy or education, let alone all three
3. When he was born in 1633 the Western world was only 100 years or so out of the renaissance

This doesn't apply only to this piece. I could have never read Epictetus without reading at least a little about the Stoics and that he was born a slave; it's all relevant. *Robinson Crusoe* is far more impressive a feat if you realize that it was the first of its kind, and not stamped out like some boilerplate romance.

Also, and this is the Philistine in me, it helps put me in the right mood. The Greek and Latin books are translated into modern(ish) English, so they are often easier to read than some of the things written in the English of hundreds of years ago. I try to imagine myself in whatever time the book was written,[44] and really try to hear the writer's voice. Oddly, the vast majority of them sound like Anthony Hopkins.

---

44. Sometimes this is easier than others. For one thing, I have a hard time with the whole "powdered wig and knee pants" thing. On the other hand, I think I'd look dashing in a Toga. To each his own.

Here's a trick: Whenever you see "eth" on the end of a word, pretend it's an "s." I'm sure purists will beat me about the head and ears for it, but if it's a choice between accomplishing the task and having my head explode like an overripe cantaloupe, so be it

Here's what I mean:

"Pride goeth before a fall…"

"Pride goes before a fall"

See? It may not be the purest reading experience, but it's much easier to understand if understanding is your goal.

Unlike Shakespeare or Milton or even (maybe especially) the King James Bible, Locke is meant to be understood and not just appreciated. Yes he writes well, but it's not designed for recreational reading, where the poetry and the phrasing are what matters. Whatever it takes to really understand what he's saying is worth doing.

Oh yeah, history. All of this is a very long way of saying that you have to know what's going on in England at the time so you can really grasp

1. the unbelievable importance and impact his religious and political writing had and how they are still valid today;
2. the unbelievable importance and impact his writings on education and child-raising had and how they screwed up 200 years of white people.

First the context: Locke was a middle-class lawyer's son who wrote as if he had a right to tell kings and the gentry what he thought. This is not a casual thing at a time when England was embroiled in a civil war, that a King's head rolled into a basket and religion was literally a matter of life and death.

It's easy for us to forget when reading his "Second Treatise on Government" or "On Tolerance" how radical the notions he raised must have seemed. Easy because many of the things he wrote are now the bedrock of liberal thinking.

Of course we accept the notion of separating church and state to at least some reasonable degree (offer void in the state of Alabama) and we can always work out the details. We recognize Locke in the writings of Rousseau, Jefferson, through reform movements in almost every country in the western world.

Think about how radical his notion of religious tolerance must have seemed. I am not naïve enough to think there was ever a time when religion didn't play a predominantly social role, it went a long way to saying who a people were and helped keep the rules out where everyone could see them. Still, back then how you chose to worship could get you imprisoned or even killed by your own countrymen.

Even a statement as unimpressive now as

> "The toleration of those that differ from others in matters of religion is so agreeable to the Gospel of Jesus Christ, and to the genuine reason of mankind, that it seems monstrous for men to be so blind as not to perceive the necessity and advantage of it in so clear a light."

Yes, for the record, that included Jews and Muslims, which is not a minor inclusion for his day, or this one come to think of it. Interestingly, the only group whose rights he didn't defend was atheists.

Locke was unable to grasp the notion of personal morality and religion not being impossibly melded together. A man without religion was a danger to himself and others. Since atheists didn't believe in a higher power, their oaths were useless, and since they had no soul to lose, couldn't be trusted as far as they could be thrown. Still, he didn't actually recommend doing them harm, which at a time when how you chose to be baptized could get your head removed from your shoulders was nothing this side of saintly.

The irony now is that his arguments are frequently used to justify removing the spiritual (and yes I think it's different than religion; give me a couple of days and I'll tell you how) element from government entirely. He'd be horrified, which I'm beginning to discover is how a great many of these writers would feel if they knew how they were misquoted or their words abused.

Or would they?

"All men are created equal" had a much different meaning in 1776 than it does today. Did Jefferson mean it when he said it? I don't think it matters nearly as much as some people would like it to. It started the ball rolling and here we are today. Words have power beyond what the speaker may mean at the moment.

Look at it this way. Einstein proved Newton wrong, but he never would have been able to find the real way time and light work if he hadn't had Newton to start with and show him the path. That's the impact Locke had on political thinking.

So, suffice it to say that I am duly impressed (like he'll sleep better as a result) by Mr. Locke and the clear-sightedness of many of his works. They aren't even that hard to read as these things go and I kept tripping over analogies today which mean

1. he's still worth reading and;
2. government hasn't gotten all that much smarter in the last 250 years.

This leads me to the next question: What the #$%^ was he thinking with some of this child-rearing and education advice?

Now in theory someone can be quite admired and still be absolutely hellacious to his own children. (Look up *Crosby, Bing* in your cosmic dictionary.)

The flyer in the book said that "many of his ideas about education became standard in England for the next 200 years." That may explain a lot.

These theories were first set out in a series of letters to Edward Clarke on how Mr. Clarke should raise his son. Some of the ideas seem incredibly farsighted for the day:

- Spare no expense on your child's tutor since they'll have a greater impact on the kid's learning than you will
- You should model/gear a kid's education to their natural temperaments and talents

- Rote learning and recitation of useless facts will kill their curiosity and wish to learn

So far so good. Then there are quotes like these:

"... since the great foundation of fear in children is pain, the way to harden and fortify children against danger is to accustom them to suffer pain..."

Does Children's Services know about this guy?

And of course there's my personal favorite:

"... for breakfast and supper, milk, milk-pottage, water-gruel, flummery[45] and twenty other things that we are wont to make in England, are very fit for children; only, in all these, let care be taken that they be plain, and without much mixture, and very sparingly seasoned with sugar, or rather none at all ... I should think that a good piece of well-made and well-baked brown bread, sometimes with, and sometimes without butter or cheese would be often the best breakfast for my young master.[46] I am sure 'tis as wholesome and will make him as strong a man as greater delicacies and if he be used to it, it will be pleasant to him. If he at any time calls for victuals between meals, use him to nothing but dry bread. If he be hungry more than wanton, bread alone will down; and if he be not hungry tis not fit he should eat."

Okay, so the Happy Meal is out of the question.

Now this does clear up a great mystery for me. I always wondered how a relatively small island, made up of (how do I put this delicately)—Englishmen—managed to conquer so much of the known world.

---

45. Flummery? I can only assume since it's listed after water-gruel it's a special kind of yummy.
46. Apparently, in an era long before indoor plumbing, feeding a kid bread and cheese two meals a day seemed like a really good idea.

Turns out they were in quest of a decent meal. Who knew?

Mind you, if you are going to train people to spend months at sea in very cramped quarters with meager rations, this is a heck of a way to start. It also helps explain the methods of schooling that created the "stiff upper lip" the British are so proud of. Yup—impervious to pain, intolerant of whining and chronically constipated is a good way to create a country ready to kick some serious colonial butt.

Now, while no one this side of the Taliban really would follow this regimen any more, it did start me thinking about my own child rearing skills. Locke's theory was to train people to endure pain and inconvenience, and not to want things they don't need. These aren't necessarily bad lessons. Do we spoil our kids too much?

I can hear my daughter now, "Duh, Dad."

I bet Locke's son (and yes, he had one—it's the first thing I looked up) never said "Duh, Dad."

Her Serene Highness is a wonderful child; warm and loving, cute as a bug's ear and really funny (which makes her way cooler than the other parent's kids, not that I'm partial). She also gets away with an awful lot of things that I never would have.

I have tried to be tougher with her, and her friends already think I'm an ogre.[47] I still find myself allowing behavior and spending money on things that I don't want to.

It's not what you think. I can stand up to my kid—mostly. There's another factor here: My daughter is unique among her friends in that she has both parents at home. My biggest parenting challenge is the other parent.

A BIG DISCLAIMER HERE: The Duchess is a terrific mother and in so many ways a far superior parent to me, as most mothers are. She is also a lot softer on the kid than I am. I can stand up to my kid—mostly. I can stand up to my wife—mostly, but like most men I have a conflict-

---

47. Not technically true. Since *Shrek* came out ogres are funny and cool. I am definitely not an ogre. Somehow that fails to comfort me.

avoidance gene that only allows me so many hills to die on.

I'm pretty sure if it was just me against the kid, I could take her at least two out of three. I can't take them both on.

How does the enlightened couple decide on these things? I think we do a pretty good job of talking these things out, all things considered. Still, when we do disagree who wins it's usually not me. Looking back at that last sentence I realized I said "wins", like it's a contest... ain't male ego a beautiful thing?

There is one thing of which I am the undisputed champ. I am universally accepted as The Heavy. I have what in the Turmel household we call, The Look. Her Serene Highness knows she's in trouble when she gets it.

Here's a discussion question: How did anyone ever shoot dirty looks before the invention of glasses? Looking over the top with the right degree of menace can stop a ravenous wolverine dead in its fuzzy tracks.

Listen closely...that sound you hear is my father howling in delighted revenge.

I'm sure part of this is revisionist history. I can remember not having some of the things my friends had and feeling hard done by. I also remember never really needing anything I didn't get. To this day I'm not sure I can tell whether I didn't get things because we couldn't afford them (more often than I probably know, not as often as I think) and when my folks decided I didn't need it and that was answer enough for you, young man.

Ultimately, it had its impact. I started working part time pretty young. I can tell you to this day how many pots of Brownie's Fried Chicken I had to cook to earn that record or that concert ticket (a concert ticket was thirty-six pots not including gas money).

My daughter just has to calculate how many times she has to ask for something before I cave. I'm not sure it's the same thing at all.

So, I find myself giving in on a lot of things my old man never would have surrendered to and not being happy about it.

I regret to say that I spend a fair amount of time seething lately. Either I'm dealing with outright insubordination, or I'm feeling ornery because things aren't done as I would have liked. I sit in the corner like some kind of patriarchal Captain Queeg, rolling steel balls in my hand and muttering about stolen strawberries.

It's a very real problem for a man of a certain age, i.e. me. Being a Neanderthal and claiming male superiority hardly seems politically correct, let alone practical. Instead of just bellowing and getting my way, I allow myself to feel frustrated and emasculated, slinking back to my cave and the relative comfort of a Cubs game.

In order to maintain peace in the kingdom, I too frequently surrender and somehow manage to refrain from becoming the lead story on the local news when The Duchess asks why my daughter acts like a spoiled brat sometimes.

I can sneer at Locke's parenting advice but somehow I get the feeling he's somewhere laughing back.

This selection is Locke's definition of what government should and shouldn't be. It doesn't sound any different (with the exception of the spelling and correct grammar) than the kind of discussion you'd hear on one of the talking-head shows today... whether that's a good thing or not is another story.

OF THE ENDS OF POLITICAL SOCIETY AND GOVERNMENT
— John Locke, from the "2nd Treatise on Government,"
1690

Sec. 123. IF man in the state of nature be so free, as has been said; if he be absolute lord of his own person and possessions, equal to the greatest, and subject to no body, why will he part with his freedom? Why will he give up this empire, and subject himself to the dominion and control of any other power? To which it is obvious to answer, that though in the state of nature he hath such a right, yet the enjoyment of it is very uncertain, and constantly exposed to the invasion of others: for all being kings as much as he, every man his equal, and the greater part no strict observers of equity and justice, the enjoyment of the property he has in this state is very unsafe, very unsecure.

This makes him willing to quit a condition, which, however free, is full of fears and continual dangers: and it is not without reason, that he seeks out, and is willing to join in society with others, who are already united, or have a mind to unite, for the mutual preservation of their lives, liberties and estates, which I call by the general name, property.

Sec. 124. THE great and chief end, therefore, of men's uniting into commonwealths, and putting themselves under government, is the preservation of their property. To which in the state of nature there are many things wanting.

First, There wants an established, settled, known law, received and allowed by common consent to be the standard of right and wrong, and the common measure to decide all controversies between them: for though the law of nature be plain and intelligible to all rational creatures; yet men being biased by their interest, as well as ignorant for want of study of it, are not apt to allow of it as a law binding to them in the application of it to their particular cases.

Sec. 125. SECONDLY, In the state of nature there wants a known and indifferent judge, with authority to determine all differences according to the established law: for every one in that state being both judge and executioner of the law of nature, men being partial to themselves, passion and revenge is very apt to carry them too far, and with too much heat, in their own cases; as well as negligence, and unconcernedness, to make them too remiss in other men's.

Sec. 126. THIRDLY, In the state of nature there often wants power to back and support the sentence when right, and to give it due execution, They who by any injustice offended, will seldom fail, where they are able, by force to make good their injustice; such resistance many times makes the punishment dangerous, and frequently destructive, to those who attempt it.

Sec. 127. THUS mankind, notwithstanding all the privileges of the state of nature, being but in an ill condition, while they remain in it, are quickly driven into society. Hence it comes to pass, that we seldom find any number of men live any time together in this state.

The inconveniencies that they are therein exposed to, by the irregular and uncertain exercise of the power every man has of punishing the transgressions of others, make them take sanctuary under the established laws of government, and therein seek the preservation of their property.

It is this makes them so willingly give up every one his single power of punishing, to be exercised by such alone, as shall be appointed to it amongst them; and by such rules as the community, or those authorized by them to that purpose, shall agree on. And in this we have the original right and rise of both the legislative and executive power, as well as of the governments and societies themselves.

Sec. 128 FOR in the state of nature, to omit the liberty he has of innocent delights, a man has two powers. The first is to do whatsoever he thinks fit for the preservation of himself, and others within the permission of the law of nature: by which law, common to them all, he and all the rest of mankind are one community, make up one society, distinct from all other creatures. And were it not for the corruption and vitiousness of degenerate men, there would be no need of any other; no necessity that men should separate from this great and natural community, and by positive agreements combine into smaller and divided associations.

The other power a man has in the state of nature, is the power to punish the crimes committed against that law. Both these he gives up, when he joins in a private, if I may so call it, or particular politic society, and incorporates into any commonwealth, separate from the rest of mankind.

Sec. 129. THE first power, viz. of doing whatsoever he thought for the preservation of himself, and the rest of mankind, he gives up to be regulated by laws made by the society, so far forth as the preservation of himself, and the rest of that hisociety shall require; which laws of the society in many things confine the liberty he had by the law of nature.

Sec. 130. SECONDLY, The power of punishing he wholly gives up, and engages his natural force, (which he might before employ in the execution of the law of nature, by his own single authority, as he thought fit) to assist the executive power of the society, as the law thereof shall require: for being now in a new state, wherein he is to enjoy many conveniences, from the labour, assistance, and society of others in the same community, as well as protection from its whole strength; he is to part also with as much of his natural liberty, in providing for himself, as the good, prosperity, and safety of the society shall require; which is not only necessary, but just, since the other members of the society do the like.

Sec. 131. BUT though men, when they enter into society, give up the equality, liberty, and executive power they had in the state of nature, into the hands of the society, to be so far disposed of by the legislative, as the good of the society shall require; yet it being only with an intention in every one the better to preserve himself, his liberty and property; (for no rational creature can be supposed to change his condition with an intention to be worse) the power of the society, or legislative constituted by them, can never be supposed to extend farther, than the common good; but is obliged to secure every one's property, by providing against those three defects above mentioned, that made the state of nature so unsafe and uneasy.

And so whoever has the legislative or supreme power of any common-wealth, is bound to govern by established standing laws, promulgated and known to the people, and not by extemporary decrees; by indifferent and upright judges, who are to decide controversies by those laws; and to employ the force of the community at home, only in the execution of such laws, or abroad to prevent or redress foreign injuries, and secure the community from inroads and invasion. And all this to be directed to no other end, but the peace, safety, and public good of the people.

ELEVEN

Schwarzenegger is an Uber-Wimp

The Iliad and The Odyssey

> Sing, O Goddess, the anger of Achilles, son of
> Peleus, that brought countless ills upon the Achaeans.
> Many a brave soul did it send hurrying down to Hades,
> and many a hero did it yild a prey to dogs and
> vultures, for so were the counsels of Zeus fulfilled
> from the day on which the son of Atreus, king of men,
> and great Achilles first fell out with one another
>
> — Homer, *The Iliad*, "Book 1,"
> (translation by Samuel Butler, 1898)

This one technically shouldn't qualify for my little experiment, I suppose. I read these in high school and kind of dug them, so I looked forward to reading them again. These were the first Classics Club volumes I ever bought so in a way I guess they are the books that started this little quest of mine.

It's appropriate, since if there were ever two books that qualified as classics, these are them. It's literally unbelievable how much of our literature can be traced to this story, the references, even our language— Achilles heel, Trojan horse, Cassandra.

They all began with this one poem,[48] credited to a blind minstrel thousands of years ago.

It's one thing to say everyone knows these characters; Odysseus and the Cyclops, or the phrases like "the face that launched a thousand ships." It's quite another to realize that for most of our civilization these were the references that literally everyone knew. Whether you were Spanish, Greek, French or English these were the first stories you heard, the first texts you studied in school and the stories you turned to for what a hero ought to be.

It's a little sad, then, that the term Trojan is mostly known now as a variety of condom. Sad, because 1) I think these stories are worth remembering; and; 2) it's the worst possible name for a form of birth control. Think about it. How did the Trojans get famous?

- ◆ They left this thing outside the city
- ◆ Soon as it got inside the wall, people came pouring out of it

Isn't that what these things are supposed to prevent?

So what are the references today that people will still understand in a thousand years—or even a hundred?

One of the hardest things when I was doing stand-up, particularly when I moved from Canada, was making sure that the cultural references were spot-on. What is a treasured icon in one area might be a punch line in another. If you don't believe me, mention Wal-Mart in the Northeast and the South. In one area it's a guaranteed laugh, in the other it's viewed as slightly less holy than Mecca.

It's hard enough in one country to settle on a reference that is instantly recognized and adopted. It's harder when you start to cross borders. Whoever said England and America were separated by a common language didn't know the half of it. One of the few fights The Duchess and I ever had was over whether or not Monty Python was

---

48. In the interest of full disclosure, I read the prose translation. I'm just not up to slogging through the poem. Call me a wimp, call me a Philistine, call me irresponsible, but there you have it.

funny.

For the record, she's still wrong, and they still are.

So what is *The Iliad* of today? *Harry Potter* has a fighting chance, and I'm actually fine with that. The test will be if "Muggles" becomes a synonym for the ordinary and bland, or a "Hagrid" becomes a code word for a biker.

It's difficult to find a true icon, especially one that truly crosses boundaries. The easy way out is to blame the postmodernists and the neo-fems and whichever other subgroup has an axe to grind, but I suspect the truth is both less complicated and more insidious than some kind of conspiracy that no one will cop to.

I have digital cable—120 channels of the best television has to offer (not a word, I'm not saying a word) broken into discreet chunks. The niches have gotten so small that you're almost guaranteed of preaching only to your own personal choir.

I think I watch more than my share of the channels; I'm a cultural omnivore. I wish I could claim some kind of moral superiority, but I think it has more to do with a total lack of attention span than any particular breadth of knowledge or taste. Even still, The Duchess and I have completely different tastes. It is conceivable (and knowing us, more than likely) that we could watch television twenty-four hours a day and never, even by accident, watch the same show at the same time.

We don't watch the same movies, except for children's films. Question: Why can adults watch 150 different movies, while kids watch the same movie 150 times. I know entire neighborhoods where the adults can recite every line of *The Lion King*.

But when Her Serene Highness gives us the chance to choose the movie, we have different tastes. My eyes can glaze over at the idea of renting a film with subtitles. The Duchess in her less charitable moods will tell you it's because my lips get tired reading them.

Even the kid's shows are broken into different blocks. There are the kids who watch the broadcast networks, almost universally known as kids whose parents can't afford cable. Then the cable watchers are split into three camps: Nickelodeon/Disney/Cartoon Network. There is some crossover, but not as much as you'd expect.

If you think this falls under the category of mildly-interesting-but-irrelevant just wait fifteen years when the Nick kids join the workforce and the Cartoon Network kids get out on parole. Trust me, you don't want to live in a world run by a generation raised on *Cow and Chicken* or *I M Weasel*, but I digress.

So the question before the court is, can we ever create a universal (or even a national) culture without sinking to an absolutely lowest common denominator, or to be more precise, making sure that culture at the very least doesn't involve Jerry Springer?

Riddle me that, Batman.

As I got into the books, it dawned on me that I remembered *The Odyssey* far better than I did *The Iliad*, maybe because there was more action and the story was much more fantastic. Still, I had forgotten how the whole Trojan War even started.

I used to think it began with Paris getting the hots for Helen and running off with the other king's wife. It's much darker than that. It seems that to the Greeks the gods were one big dysfunctional family who used human beings as pawns in their little reindeer games.

Exhibit A: apparently Zeus could have put a stop to the whole war except he was afraid of his wife.

Allow me to make sure I have this:

Thetis is Achilles' mother. She's having an affair with Zeus under the theory that if you're going to sleep with married men, you may as well go after big game. Achilles is the greatest hero of the Greek army, and Zeus would like the Greeks to win for her sake, but that might tip off Hera (Mrs. Zeus) so he keeps playing off one side against the other. To me this seems just a tad passive-aggressive. Zeus makes Bill Clinton look like a tower of integrity in comparison.

The thing about the books, though, is that throughout the gods are seen as capricious, emotionally stunted and more than a little childish.

It's a great soap opera really:

- Zeus is cheating on Hera who…
- asks Apollo to help her but…
- Apollo is having a feud with his sister Athena…
- meanwhile, Poseidon has it in for Odysseus who may or may not have had an affair with...
- Athena, who is messing with…
- Achilles who's pouting over the death of his male lover…

Well, you get the point. With gods like this, it's no wonder the Stoics emerged. Think about it. If the gods were all in competition, and you never knew what any of them would do at any given time, and everything is out of your control, then you may as well shut up and deal with it.

Fast forward 3,000 years and you have one God, with a slightly better attitude, but it's still largely "do it *my* way and nobody gets hurt."

The Stoics still have a point. Funny how I keep going back there. Hmmmmmm.

And then there's the whole notion of war and adventure stories in general. The earliest recorded stories were about war or some other violent confrontation.

We've always admired the warrior. Bravery and some kind of code, whether chivalry or just the soldier's code (whatever the heck that is) make him a person to be admired, to model yourself after. Think of the great characters of literature: from Gilgamesh and David to Jason, Beowulf, Arthur and Roland to D'Artagnan, Jim Hawkins and Scaramouche to Jack Ryan and Spencer (the guy for hire, not the poet, who according to all accounts punched like a girl). All are paragons to be admired.

So what kind of heroes do we find in the Trojan War and the Odyssey that followed? Let's see:

There's Achilles. He seems to have been at least bisexual, but since he was the best all-around fighter the Greeks had it pretty much kibashes the whole "gays in the military" argument. No, the problem with him is that he felt hard done by because a fellow king kept a beautiful slave girl that should have been his. Whether he wanted the woman or not seems to be irrelevant because he then began the longest and bloodiest holdout since Eric Lindros stiffed the Philadelphia Flyers. It wasn't until his best friend/lover dies in battle that he rejoins the war. Several massacres and violations of the Geneva convention later, he is ultimately killed himself.

Then there's Odysseus. He's a renowned liar, sneak and all-around no-goodnik. His main virtues seem to be that he's a great wrestler and was the brains behind the Trojan Horse. I also question his sailing skills, since it took twenty years to get from Troy to Ithaca (on modern day Sicily). Three Boy Scouts in a kayak could do that trip in a month.[49]

So throughout the classics—and even the trash I'm more accustomed to reading—the warrior is celebrated and held up as the model for all young boys to aspire to. When did that change?

We still talk a good game when it comes to the military, and the Tom Clancys of the world attempt to keep the tradition alive, but it sounds vaguely hollow and anachronistic.

What happened, I think, was the camera. Before the Crimean War in the 1840s, the only record of battles or what war was like was either by poets and minstrels who were paid to tell a good story, or by the survivors, who more often than not were paying the minstrels. According to the old adage by Senator Hiram Warren Johnson, "the first casualty when war comes is truth." That makes war a lot like bass fishing; mostly done by men, not appreciated by non participants and the facts never get in the way of a good story.

By the time the Boer War arrived, it was harder to hide the truth about what war and violence were really like. Cameras got smaller, and a relatively free press began to show the truth about battle scenes. The

---

49. See also Moses et al taking forty years to get from Egypt to Israel. You can hike that in a weekend if you start early enough. Apparently along with the tablets he should have asked the Almighty for a map.

ugly reality, mixed with the fact that the Boer war was really hard to justify in the first place—it was between two groups of white people, neither of which had any decent claim to the land in the first place—and was an embarrassment to the British (they were getting their butts handed to them by a bunch of Dutch farmers.[50]

Some of the outcry was political, of course. The Socialists had begun to make inroads and were far more effective than the Christian churches that had continued to resist the government. Jaures and others had the notion that the workers of the world shouldn't fight each other. Why that seemed to hold more water than the idea that Christians shouldn't kill each other is beyond me, maybe because there were more workers.

Maybe it was technology. I can actually see the romance and glory when war consisted of two sides, both with swords or spears and looking each other in the eye. The strongest, smartest guy with the best sword hand stayed alive and looked pretty cool doing it—think Errol Flynn. When one guy with a machine gun could take out dozens of men without ever having to see their faces, the game changed drastically.

Maybe that's why I don't and won't own a gun, but I do fence and have a sword. It's not that one is morally superior to the other, I just figure it's cooler.

So, I'm not so much a pacifist as a military Luddite. There's a comforting thought.

By WWI the game had changed dramatically. The fact that people could actually get a sense for themselves of how horrible war was didn't help its reputation any. Fortunately, every once in a while a Hitler would come along and revive the notion of a "good war."

So where does that leave us today? On the one hand we admire pacifism if it's of the noble type (Jaures, Gandhi, Martin Luther King) and not the appeasing type (Chamberlin, Bud Selig). On the other, it's

---

50. It wasn't so embarrassing to be beaten by farmers, 1776 prepared them for that, but who the #$%^ gets beaten by the Dutch?

hard not to admire the soldier or noble adventurer. After all, action movies still do big business and probably always will.

By the way, my hypocrisy meter won't let me go without saying I love action movies. Yes, they can become horribly depressing especially when well done (if I see *Black Hawk Down* again, it will be because I've been caged like a veal and forced to sit through it. Good movie; Ridley Scott directed his butt off, don't make me go through that again please) but I can tell the difference between real violence and pretend. I'm also not one to say things have gotten worse over time. *The Odyssey* ends with Odysseus and his son Telemachus personally massacring (by bow and sword mind you, not bomb or machine gun) dozens of men:

> "Meanwhile, Odysseus, as long as his arrows lasted, had been shooting the suitors one by one, and they fell thick on one another. When his arrows gave out, he set the bow to stand against the end wall of the house by the doorpost, and hung a shield four hides thick about his shoulders; on his comely head he set his helmet, well wrought with a crest of horsehair that nodded menacingly above it, and he grasped two redoubtable bronze-shod spears."

Action like that makes Schwarzenegger in the last reel of *Commando* look like some kind of Uber-Wimp. Real men don't need Uzis.

So how does an intelligent, aware, more or less politically correct person enjoy stories with such violence?

A whole bunch, thank you.

How do you reconcile that?

Don't think too hard.

I picked this chapter of *The Odyssey* because it contains all the elements we still see in adventure movies to this day: wily hero, bloody action, a babe who falls in love with the hero for no apparent reason, and men who turn into pigs. I know, I know, write your own joke, I'm tired.

THE ODYSSEY
— Homer (translated by Samuel Butler, 1867)

Chapter 10

..."When they reached Circe's house they found it built of cut stones, on a site that could be seen from far, in the middle of the forest. There were wild mountain wolves and lions prowling all round it—poor bewitched creatures whom she had tamed by her enchantments and drugged into subjection. They did not attack my men, but wagged their great tails, fawned upon them, and rubbed their noses lovingly against them. As hounds crowd round their master when they see him coming from dinner—for they know he will bring them something—even so did these wolves and lions with their great claws fawn upon my men, but the men were terribly frightened at seeing such strange creatures.

Presently they reached the gates of the goddess's house, and as they stood there they could hear Circe within, singing most beautifully as she worked at her loom, making a web so fine, so soft, and of such dazzling colours as no one but a goddess could weave.

On this Polites, whom I valued and trusted more than any other of my men, said, 'There is some one inside working at a loom and singing most beautifully; the whole place resounds with it, let us call her and see whether she is woman or goddess.'

"They called her and she came down, unfastened the door, and bade them enter. They, thinking no evil, followed her, all except Eurylochus, who suspected mischief and stayed outside. When she had got them into her house, she set them upon benches and seats and mixed them a mess with cheese, honey, meal, and Pramnian but she drugged it with wicked poisons to make them forget their homes, and when they had drunk she turned them into pigs by a stroke of her wand, and shut them up in her pigsties. They were like pigs-head, hair, and all, and they grunted just as pigs do; but their senses were the same as before, and they remembered everything

"Thus then were they shut up squealing, and Circe threw them some acorns and beech masts such as pigs eat, but Eurylochus hurried back to tell me about the sad fate of our comrades. He was so overcome with dismay that though he tried to speak he could find no words to do so; his eyes filled with tears and he could only sob and sigh, till at last we forced his story out of him, and he told us what had happened to the others.

"'We went,' said he, as you told us, through the forest, and in the middle of it there was a fine house built with cut stones in a place that could be seen from far. There we found a woman, or else she was a goddess, working at her loom and singing sweetly; so the men shouted to her and called her, whereon she at once came down, opened the door, and invited us in. The others did not suspect any mischief so they followed her into the house, but I stayed where I was, for I thought there might be some treachery. From that moment I saw them no more, for not one of them ever came out, though I sat a long time watching for them.'

"Then I took my sword of bronze and slung it over my shoulders; I also took my bow, and told Eurylochus to come back with me and show me the way. But he laid hold of me with both his hands and spoke piteously, saying, 'Sir, do not force me to go with you, but let me stay here, for I know you will not bring one of them back with you nor even return alive yourself; let us rather see if we cannot escape at any rate with the few that are left us, for we may still save our lives.'

"'Stay where you are, then,' answered I, 'eating and drinking at the ship, but I must go, for I am most urgently bound to do so.'

"With this I left the ship and went up inland. When I got through the charmed grove, and was near the great house of the enchantress Circe, I met Mercury with his golden wand, disguised as a young man in the hey-day of his youth and beauty with the down just coming upon his face. He came up to me and took my hand within his own, saying, 'My poor unhappy man, whither are you going over this mountain top, alone and without knowing the way? Your men are shut up in Circe's pigsties, like so many wild boars in their lairs. You surely do not fancy that you can set them free? I can tell you that you will never get back and will have to stay there with the rest of them. But never mind, I will protect you and get you out of your difficulty. Take this herb, which is one of great virtue, and keep it about you when you go to Circe's house, it will be a talisman to you against every kind of mischief.

"'And I will tell you of all the wicked witchcraft that Circe will try to practise upon you.[51] She will mix a mess for you to drink, and she will drug the meal with which she makes it, but she will not be able to charm you, for the virtue of the herb that I shall give you will prevent her spells from working. I will tell you all about it. When Circe strikes you with her wand, draw your sword and spring upon her as though you were going to kill her. She will then be frightened and will desire you to go to bed with her; on this you must not point blank refuse her, for you want her to set your companions free, and to take good care also of yourself, but you make her swear solemnly by all the blessed that she will plot no further mischief against you, or else when she has got you naked she will unman you and make you fit for nothing.'

"As he spoke he pulled the herb out of the ground an showed me what it was like. The root was black, while the flower was as white as milk; the gods call it Moly, and mortal men cannot uproot it, but the gods can do whatever they like.

"Then Mercury went back to high Olympus passing over the wooded island; but I fared onward to the house of Circe, and my heart was clouded with care as I walked along. When I got to the gates I stood there and called the goddess, and as soon as she heard me she came down, opened the door, and asked me to come in; so I followed her—much troubled in my mind. She set

---

51. We all know, if you really want to get the dirt on someone, talk to their ex. Nothing's changed.

me on a richly decorated seat inlaid with silver, there was a footstool also under my feet, and she mixed a mess in a golden goblet for me to drink; but she drugged it, for she meant me mischief. When she had given it to me, and I had drunk it without its charming me, she struck me with her wand. 'There now,' she cried, 'be off to the pigsty, and make your lair with the rest of them.'

"But I rushed at her with my sword drawn as though I would kill her, whereon she fell with a loud scream, clasped my knees, and spoke piteously, saying, 'Who and whence are you? From what place and people have you come? How can it be that my drugs have no power to charm you? Never yet was any man able to stand so much as a taste of the herb I gave you; you must be spell-proof; surely you can be none other than the bold hero Ulysses, who Mercury always said would come here some day with his ship while on his way home form Troy; so be it then; sheathe your sword and let us go to bed, that we may make friends and learn to trust each other.'

"And I answered, 'Circe, how can you expect me to be friendly with you when you have just been turning all my men into pigs? And now that you have got me here myself, you mean me mischief when you ask me to go to bed with you, and will unman me and make me fit for nothing. I shall certainly not consent to go to bed with you unless you will first take your solemn oath to plot no further harm against me.'

"So she swore at once as I had told her, and when she had completed her oath then I went to bed with her.

"Meanwhile her four servants, who are her housemaids, set about their work. They are the children of the groves and fountains, and of the holy waters that run down into the sea. One of them spread a fair purple cloth over a seat, and laid a carpet underneath it. Another brought tables of silver up to the seats, and set them with baskets of gold. A third mixed some sweet wine with water in a silver bowl and put golden cups upon the tables, while the fourth she brought in water and set it to boil in a large cauldron over a good fire which she had lighted. When the water in the cauldron was boiling, she poured cold into it till it was just as I liked it, and then she set me in a bath and began washing me from the cauldron about the head and shoulders, to take the tire and stiffness out of my limbs. As soon as she had done washing me and anointing me with oil, she arrayed me in a good cloak and shirt and led me to a richly decorated seat inlaid with silver; there was a footstool also under my feet. A maid servant then brought me water in a beautiful golden ewer and poured it into a silver basin for me to wash my hands, and she drew a clean table beside me; an upper servant brought me bread and offered me many things of what there was in the house, and then Circe bade me eat, but I would not, and sat without heeding what was before me, still moody and suspicious.

"When Circe saw me sitting there without eating, and in great grief, she came to me and said, 'Ulysses, why do you sit like that as though you were dumb, gnawing at your own heart, and refusing both meat and drink? Is it that you are still suspicious? You ought not to be, for I have already sworn solemnly that I will not hurt you.'

"And I said, 'Circe, no man with any sense of what is right can think of either eating or drinking in your house until you have set his friends free and let him see them. If you want me to eat and drink, you must free my men and bring them to me that I may see them with my own eyes.'

"When I had said this she went straight through the court with her wand in her hand and opened the pigsty doors. My men came out like so many prime hogs and stood looking at her, but she went about among them and anointed each with a second drug, whereon the bristles that the bad drug had given them fell off, and they became men again, younger than they were before, and much taller and better looking. They knew me at once, seized me each of them by the hand, and wept for joy till the whole house was filled with the sound of their hullabalooing, and Circe herself was so sorry for them that she came up to me and said, 'Ulysses, noble son of Laertes, go back at once to the sea where you have left your ship, and first draw it on to the land. Then, hide all your ship's gear and property in some cave, and come back here with your men.'

"I agreed to this, so I went back to the sea shore, and found the men at the ship weeping and wailing most piteously. When they saw me the silly blubbering fellows began frisking round me as calves break out and gambol round their mothers, when they see them coming home to be milked after they have been feeding all day, and the homestead resounds with their lowing. They seemed as glad to see me as though they had got back to their own rugged Ithaca, where they had been born and bred. 'Sir,' said the affectionate creatures, 'we are as glad to see you back as though we had got safe home to Ithaca; but tell us all about the fate of our comrades.'

"I spoke comfortingly to them and said, 'We must draw our ship on to the land, and hide the ship's gear with all our property in some cave; then come with me all of you as fast as you can to Circe's house, where you will find your comrades eating and drinking in the midst of great abundance.'

"On this the men would have come with me at once, but Eurylochus tried to hold them back and said, 'Alas, poor wretches that we are, what will become of us? Rush not on your ruin by going to the house of Circe, who will turn us all into pigs or wolves or lions, and we shall have to keep guard over her house. Remember how the Cyclops treated us when our comrades went inside his cave, and Ulysses with them. It was all through his sheer folly that those men lost their lives.'

"When I heard him I was in two minds whether or no to draw the keen blade that hung by my sturdy thigh and cut his head off in spite of his being a near relation of my own; but the men interceded for him and said, 'Sir, if it may so be, let this fellow stay here and mind the ship, but take the rest of us with you to Circe's house.'

"On this we all went inland, and Eurylochus was not left behind after all, but came on too, for he was frightened by the severe reprimand that I had given him.

"Meanwhile Circe had been seeing that the men who had been left behind were washed and anointed with olive oil; she had also given them woollen cloaks and shirts, and when we came we found them all comfortably at dinner in her house. As soon as the men saw each other face to face and knew one another, they wept for joy and cried aloud till the whole palace rang again. Thereon Circe came up to me and said, 'Ulysses, noble son of Laertes, tell your men to leave off crying; I know how much you have all of you suffered at sea, and how ill you have fared among cruel savages on the mainland, but that is over now, so stay here, and eat and drink till you are once more as strong and hearty as you were when you left Ithaca; for at present you are weakened both in body and mind; you keep all the time thinking of the hardships you have suffered during your travels, so that you have no more cheerfulness left in you.'

"Thus did she speak and we assented. We stayed with Circe for a whole twelvemonth feasting upon an untold quantity both of meat and wine. But when the year had passed in the waning of moons and the long days had come round, my men called me apart and said, 'Sir, it is time you began to think about going home, if so be you are to be spared to see your house and native country at all.'

"Thus did they speak and I assented. Thereon through the livelong day to the going down of the sun we feasted our fill on meat and wine, but when the sun went down and it came on dark the men laid themselves down to sleep in the covered cloisters. I, however, after I had got into bed with Circe, besought her by her knees, and the goddess listened to what I had got to say. 'Circe,' said I, 'please to keep the promise you made me about furthering me on my homeward voyage. I want to get back and so do my men, they are always pestering me with their complaints as soon as ever your back is turned.'

"And the goddess answered, 'Ulysses, noble son of Laertes, you shall none of you stay here any longer if you do not want to, but there is another journey which you have got to take before you can sail homewards...'[52]

---

52. Yeah, there's always one more thing... The Duchess does that to me too.

TWELVE

Would It Kill You to Smile a Little?

Plays of Henrik Ibsen

> SOLNESS: The luck will turn. I know it—I feel the day approaching. Some one or other will take it into his head to say: Give me a chance! And then all the rest will come clamouring after him, and shake their fists at me and shout: Make room- make room- make room! Yes, just you see, Doctor—presently the younger generation will come knocking at my door.
>
> DR. H *(laughing)*: Well, and what if they do?
>
> SOLNESS: What if they do? Then there's an end of Halvard Solness.
>
> —Henrik Ibsen, *The Master Builder*, 1873

Okay, what do I know about Henrik Ibsen?

- He was Norwegian
- His plays are famous for being bleak and depressing
- I've never seen one because of... well, 1 and 2

A couple of other things I know:

- Hedda Gabler is one of those parts that young starlets tell interviewers they're dying to play some day when they take a break from making Bikini Carwash IV

- ♦ They haven't read it either

Anything I know about Ibsen I learned from The Duchess. She was a for-real actress for twenty years, making a living without a day job for much of that time, at least until three margaritas and a wayward sperm put a big crimp in her career. She told me I'd love Ibsen.

She also told me I'd love the new duvet she got at TJ Maxx so I should have been suspicious right there.[53] Maybe the people who love Ibsen are the same people who spend $300 on a set of bedding. This I do know: I ain't one of them.

Somehow the notion of putting out good money for pillows my head is not permitted to touch, bedcovers I will be murdered for spilling chocolate ice cream on and, best of all, $45 a set for something called a "sham" (which may be the greatest example of truth in advertising I've seen in some time) doesn't inspire anything resembling love. Neither does an evening of people named Hedwig and Torvald discussing madness, infidelity, and the brain-softening effects of syphilis.

I don't know why I don't go to plays more often. I have always followed theater, read the reviews in the paper, watched interviews with playwrights, been forced at knifepoint to watch the Tony awards once a year—that kind of thing. Heck I was even a drama geek in high school, but if I had to count the number of professional plays I've seen in my life, the number is embarrassingly low.

Remove Broadway-type musicals from that list and I'm down to less than a dozen, a list which includes a thinly disguised version of *Hamlet* set in a Viking village, the tender tale of a homosexual skinhead who stomps a priest to death, and *Charles Manson: the Musical*. I make none of this up.

That's one problem with theatre, of course, is that there is so much

---

53. For the benefit of straight male readers: A duvet (pronounced doovay) is a bedspread, only less comfortable and more expensive, or so I'm told.

of it that's just god-awful. It's one thing to pay $9 to watch some lame picture with Tiffany Tori Amber Jennifer Love Geller. Hey, you munch your popcorn, you sit in the air-conditioning and she can't hear you wonder out loud what happened to leading ladies with real hooters. It's quite another problem when you're one of twelve people in an over-heated, Equity-waiver church basement sitting on hard wooden folding chairs watching some Starbucks barista try to get his pierced tongue around Tartuffe.

Bang for the buck is definitely a problem here. Remember, we're a suburban couple with a nine-year-old:

- Tickets anywhere from $30-75 a pair (make that closer to $100 if it's a play you've actually heard of)
- Parking $10
- Baby-sitter $20
- Pizza for kid and baby-sitter $20
- Drinks so that we can justify leaving the house and paying a baby-sitter $20

When I watch a movie, that's not a real person up there. When I'm sitting in a theater, I can't get past the fact that there's a real person up there. When they are good, it can tear your heart out. When they're not, well, it can tear your heart out.

And what about Ibsen's plays as entertainment? They're not for the faint of heart. Never mind that they are a nonstop barrage of Torvalds and Lundefisks, being Norwegian there isn't much help for that. They are, however, full of long speeches and short on action, except at the end of every second play when someone shoots themselves.

The speeches set up the issues, which is what the plays are really about. Ibsen was about something, a reaction to most plays of the time (heck of any time that I can see) which were mostly romantic melodramas (think of them as real-time chick flicks). Give him points, he's about something alright. Here are the main themes I've been able to pull out of his plays:

- Women are undervalued—except when they're potential for destruction is underestimated
- Conformity is valued more by the middle class than individual initiative or talent (not too self-serving a notion for the admittedly precocious and highly individual child of a Norwegian timber merchant)
- Syphilis is bad (going wayyyyy out on a limb there, but he does get points for at least mentioning the topic, if not actually saying the words)

Make no mistake, these are not feel-good teenage romps. We're talking Oscar-seeking, Morrissey-song, Sylvia-Plath-poem, hide-the-razor-blades, I-wonder-how-long-it-will-take-to-find-my-rotted-carcass, they'll-all-be-sorry-then depressing.

Part of my discomfort might come at my identification with the themes, particularly the fear of financial ruin. Suicide over the threat of bankruptcy is, to us, a seemingly quaint notion. To Ibsen it was real, having watched his father's career destroyed when he was still young.

Now, Chapters 7-13 allow us to escape the "stranglehold of debt" and start over. Never mind how you got in trouble in the first place or whether you actually learned anything.

I know from whence I speak. We went through a bankruptcy five years ago, and while on the surface it was the best thing for everyone concerned (with the possible exception of the people to whom we owed the money), I have gone through staring at the ceiling in the dead of night doing that "total life insurance – bills = can I make it look like an accident?" math problem.

What have I learned from it? Not much really, except a Scarlett O'Hara-like resolve that it will...not...happen...again.

I'm not entirely sure that The Duchess learned the same lesson, but at least from reading Ibsen I now have a literary reference (God bless the classics) to draw on when I have to tell her, "For the last time, Hedda, the bill is due when it's on white paper. The red notices do not mean, Oh good, it's time to pay this one now."

Frankly, I got off pretty lucky. Society has forgiven the financially incompetent, which for most of us is good news, even if it eliminates the option of putting Ken Lay, Bernie Ebbers and the guy from Global Crossing in a locked room with a loaded pistol and saving the SEC a lot of time and trouble.

Moreover I don't know what's more depressing: the subject matter or the fact that 100 years after they were written the questions he raises are still valid. Go ahead and tell me that we value the truly original thinker, that women, particularly in the home, are valued, or that syphilis is good. The only good news there is that there are now things that are worse. Not exactly warm comfort.

Worse, I suppose, is that not only are the themes still relevant but they are so openly discussed now (not solved, just discussed) that they are the stuff of soap operas and sitcoms:

"Tonight on *Just Shoot Me*[54] Finch has a wacky mix-up at the free clinic, and Nina's illegitimate daughter shows up in time for the magazine's family picnic, giving her a partner for the three-legged race."

At least laughing is one way to address a problem, maybe the best one. George Bernard Shaw once said, "If you're going to tell people the truth, make them laugh or they'll kill you," and there's something to that. Comedians die of old age: George Burns was over 100. Bob Hope is close; Don Rickles is eighty years old if you need further proof. Prophets die young (Jesus was thirty-three) and poets and playwrights kill themselves early so people thing they're prophets.

I often wonder how far religion would have gotten if it didn't take itself so seriously. What if Jesus really had said, "Hey Peter, I can see your house from here."[55] What if the parables started with, "Two apostles walk into a bar…"

---

54. To my knowledge the first sitcom named for the audience's reaction to having watched it. See also *Les Miserables* for its Broadway counterpart.
55. It's the punch line to an old joke. If you don't know it, ask your nearest pastor or priest. I guarantee they know it.

I mean you have to be pretty serious to want to convert the entire world to your point of view, but lightening up a bit would probably help. I can't help imagining some sun-kissed, semi-naked, polygamous native on a south sea island watching these over-dressed, uptight, obviously miserable, malarial, sweaty white people and thinking to myself, "Oh yeah, where do I sign up for this?"

The closest Ibsen gets to a laugh is in *Enemy of the People*, when, after something he says at a town meeting incites a riot and he escapes with his clothes torn, Dr. Stockmann says, "Wear two pairs of pants if you're going to tell them the truth." This may be one of the more brilliant lines in literature if you look at it closely enough. Lord knows that one will find its way into a company newsletter at some point.

The good news for those of us who've never read plays as literature is that it's really an easy read. Anything written in the last 200 years is easy to follow and get through quickly.

Think about it, a script is only plot and dialogue. This person says this, that person says that, they move to the table and sit down. Compare that to a novel where you'd get their inner thoughts, a description of their eyebrows and the table as a metaphor for the deck of a ship or some nuttiness. A perfect example is Victor Hugo, who in *Les Miserables* will have Jean Valjean escape into a nunnery, then we get thirty pages of description and history on the convent before he's heard of again. Think of reading plays as "Classic Literature for Dummies."

I've actually read a number of plays this way since I've read Ibsen, and it's a great time-saver if nothing else. Think about it: the average play lasts a couple of hours including intermission. Even the slowest reader can finish a script in less time than that, and if it does happen to take a while, well think of it as being able to put the actors on "pause" while you take a potty break.

All this brings me back to the fundamental question: Did I like the plays? The facile answer is, *Master Builder* and *Enemy of the People*— yes; *A Doll's House*—sort of; and *Hedda Gabler* and *The Wild Duck*— hell no.

The closest analogy I can think of was about a week ago when The Duchess wanted to rent a movie called, *The Anniversary Party*. It starred a pretty good cast including Jennifer Jason Leigh, one of my favorite actresses despite being blonde and normal-looking which is seldom my fantasy type. (Okay, I'll admit it. She turns me on because she falls into the category of "truly, deeply, dangerously crazy," which I find sexy as hell.)

The acting was uniformly excellent.

The story was heartbreaking.

Despite a miniscule budget, the film was well made and edited

If I sit through it again, it will be because I've been duct-taped to a chair and my eyes held open *Clockwork Orange* style. Divorce, drug abuse, infidelity, public disgrace, naked emotional attacks. That was fun, mommy, can we do that again?

Fact is, the script would have made an excellent play, but if I begrudge the $1.99 I paid for the video rental (I had a coupon), my desire to pay $30 to watch the emotional carnage is severely limited, I guarantee you.

See, I get the high cost of Broadway musicals for the most part. Big production budgets, talented, pretty people at the top of their craft, I get that. *Oklahoma, The Producers*—you laugh, you leave singing, it's all about value, as the song says.

On the other hand, what's with Stephen Sondheim and his ilk? When did Broadway musicals become these dark angst-filled productions? How do you get a happy ending out of *Titanic? Miss Saigon? Sweeney* @#$%^!^ *Todd* for crying out loud?

Of course, I don't understand why someone would do heroin either. "Give me something that will make me sleepy and nauseous—in no particular order." At least with cocaine or acid there is at least a euphoria and the outside shot at having a reasonably good time. At least, that's what I've heard. I didn't inhale. Go ask your mother.

I ain't no theater critic, but to me Ibsen belongs in that category of writers like Eugene O'Neill (alcoholism, drug addiction, insanity) and Tennessee Williams (all of the above plus sexual dysfunction and cannibalism—what a fun date this guy must have been) who wrote brilliant work worth watching. I qualify this by saying that in the hands of a great cast you are pulled in, identify with the characters and are amazed at the talent on display. In the wrong hands, you envy Sebastian from, *Suddenly, Last Summer*, his death, if only because it happened before the play started. Ripped apart and eaten by the street children you were molesting is preferable to bad agenda theater, believe me.

Here's a scene from *An Enemy of the People*, by Ibsen. The town doctor has just found out that the city's main tourist attraction is pestilent and should be closed down. ("We can't close the beaches, Sheriff, Amity depends on the fourth of July weekend..." Think of this as what sheriff Brody in *Jaws* would have gone through if the shark had stopped at one swimmer and Robert Shaw hadn't been available.)

An Enemy of the People
— Henrik Ibsen, 1876

Act 1

MRS. STOCKMANN. Then that is what you have been so busy with?

DR. STOCKMANN. Indeed I have been busy, Katherine. But here I had none of the necessary scientific apparatus; so I sent samples, both of the drinking-water and of the sea-water, up to the University, to have an accurate analysis made by a chemist.

HOVSTAD. And have you got that?

DR. STOCKMANN (*showing him the letter*). Here it is! It proves the presence of decomposing organic matter in the water—it is full of infusoria. The water is absolutely dangerous to use, either internally or externally.

MRS. STOCKMANN. What a mercy you discovered it in time.

DR. STOCKMANN. You may well say so.

HOVSTAD. And what do you propose to do now, Doctor?

DR. STOCKMANN. To see the matter put right, naturally.

HOVSTAD. Can that be done?

DR. STOCKMANN. It must be done. Otherwise the Baths will be absolutely useless and wasted. But we need not anticipate that; I have a very clear idea what we shall have to do.

MRS. STOCKMANN. But why have you kept this all so secret, dear?

DR. STOCKMANN. Do you suppose I was going to run about the town gossiping about it, before I had absolute proof? No, thank you. I am not such a fool.

PETRA. Still, you might have told us—

DR. STOCKMANN. Not a living soul. But tomorrow you may run around to the old Badger—

MRS. STOCKMANN. Oh, Thomas! Thomas!

DR. STOCKMANN. Well, to your grandfather, then. The old boy will have something to be astonished at! I know he thinks I am cracked—and there are lots of other people who think so too, I have noticed. But now these good folks shall see—they shall just see! (*Walks about, rubbing his hands.*) There will be a nice upset in the town, Katherine; you can't imagine what it will be. All the conduit-pipes will have to be relaid.

HOVSTAD (*getting up*). All the conduit-pipes—?

DR. STOCKMANN. Yes, of course. The intake is too low down; it will have to be lifted to a position much higher up.

PETRA. Then you were right after all.

DR. STOCKMANN. Ah, you remember, Petra—I wrote opposing the plans before the work was begun. But at that time no one would listen to me. Well, I am going to let them have it now. Of course I have prepared a report for the Baths Committee; I have had it ready for a week, and was only waiting for this to come. (*Shows the letter.*) Now it shall go off at once. (*Goes into his room and comes back with some papers.*) Look at that! Four closely written sheets!—and the letter shall go with them. Give me a bit of paper, Katherine—something to wrap them up in. That will do! Now give it to-to-(*stamps his foot*)—what the deuce is her name?—give it to the maid, and tell her to take it at once to the Mayor.

(*Mrs. Stockmann takes the packet and goes out through the dining-room.*)

PETRA. What do you think Uncle Peter will say, father?

DR. STOCKMANN. What is there for him to say? I should think he would be very glad that such an important truth has been brought to light.[56]

HOVSTAD. Will you let me print a short note about your discovery in the "Messenger?

DR. STOCKMANN. I shall be very much obliged if you will.

HOVSTAD. It is very desirable that the public should be informed of it without delay.

---

56. Oh yeah, that'll work. Mayors love that kind of news. The poor doctor never had a chance to see *Silkwood* or *The Informer*.

DR. STOCKMANN. Certainly.

MRS. STOCKMANN *(coming back)*. She has just gone with it.

BILLING. Upon my soul, Doctor, you are going to be the foremost man in the town!

DR. STOCKMANN *(walking about happily)*. Nonsense! As a matter of fact I have done nothing more than my duty. I have only made a lucky find—that's all. Still, all the same...

BILLING. Hovstad, don't you think the town ought to give Dr. Stockmann some sort of testimonial?

HOVSTAD. I will suggest it, anyway.

BILLING. And I will speak to Aslaksen about it.

DR. STOCKMANN. No, my good friends, don't let us have any of that nonsense. I won't hear anything of the kind. And if the Baths Committee should think of voting me an increase of salary, I will not accept it. Do you hear, Katherine?—I won't accept it.

MRS. STOCKMANN. You are quite right, Thomas.

PETRA *(lifting her glass)*. Your health, father!

HOVSTAD AND BILLING. Your health, Doctor! Good health!

HORSTER *(touches glasses with Dr. Stockmann)*. I hope it will bring you nothing but good luck.

DR. STOCKMANN. Thank you, thank you, my dear fellows! I feel tremendously happy! It is a splendid thing for a man to be able to feel that he has done a service to his native town and to his fellow-citizens. Hurrah, Katherine! *(He puts his arms round her and whirls her round and round, while she protests with laughing cries. They all laugh, clap their hands, and cheer the DOCTOR. The boys put their heads in at the door to see what is going on.)*

We know this is early in the play because the boys are happy and everyone is convinced it will turn out all right. Soon the paper doesn't want to carry the story, people are concerned for their jobs and the doctor is threatened with having to move to America (and before you think that's not so bad, let's not forget that Norwegians wind up in Minneapolis or Duluth, not Los Angeles or Miami) to escape the literal and probably physical stench.

At least this one doesn't end with a gunshot; the doctor is only a pariah, unemployable, deserted by everyone in town and probably crazy, so it's as close to a happy ending as Ibsen ever wrote.

THIRTEEN

How to Talk Dirty and Influence 400 Years of Writers

Essays of Montaigne

> As I was considering the way a painter I employ went about his work, I had a mind to imitate him. He chooses the best spot, the middle of each wall, for a picture labored over with all his skill, and the empty space all around it he fills with grotesques, which are fantastic paintings whose only charm lies in their variety and strangeness. And what are these essays, in truth, but grotesques and monstrous bodies, pieced together of divers members, without definite shape, having no order, sequence, or proportion other than accidental?
>
> —Michel de Montaigne, "Of Friendship," 1580
> (translated by Donald M. Frame)

I'm on a bit of a roll here. Reading these books has been more fun, much less of a chore than I had expected. I'm constantly surprised to discover that for the most part they have something to say, or at least get me thinking about things going on in my life.

More importantly, I think there's this weird tingly feeling—or

146

maybe thrill is the right word—when I uncover something that simply rings true.

I don't expect anyone to believe this, but just as I wrote that last line I came across this one:

> "Still, I am pleased at this, that my opinions have the honor of often coinciding with theirs, and that at least I go the same way, though far behind them saying, 'How true'. Also that I have this—which not everyone has—that I know the vast difference between them and me." — "Of the Education of Children"

No @#$% Sherlock. This, after all is what much of this experiment of mine has been about: to hear what those who came before me had to say; to figure out why they were so much smarter than I am. What I'm finding is that I agree with many of them. Does that mean I'm as smart as they are? No and heck no, but it does mean maybe I'm not as dumb as I thought I was.

The truth is out there and every once in a while you stumble over it. "Even a blind pig finds an acorn once in a while" my old boss used to say. Yeah, but did he recognize it when he found it and know what to do with it?

What's a guy supposed to do with this stuff once he uncovers it? I really thought when I read something that blew me away, I was supposed to buy it completely, follow it, and all of a sudden I would be a follower of Epictetus or whoever, and if I didn't somehow I wasn't really committed to what they had to say and the problem was with me. Instead, I am beginning to believe that, to overdo a metaphor, when you pan for gold you keep the nuggets and toss the rest.

How do I know when I find gold? You just know, and you slide that one into your pocket and move on

That certainly wasn't the way many of these books were originally written. They were prescriptive—do this or that. I know the way and if you don't follow it you're not as good/smart/all-around wonderful as I am.

Still, I do confess to getting a wonderfully smug feeling when I stumble over something I have always thought but couldn't quite articulate. How pathetic is that? Montaigne (or Plato, or Lucretius or whomever) said it so it must bet true. Since I believe that too, I am in the same league as these guys. Somewhat comforting until you realize that's really the literary equivalent of choosing a Chinese restaurant because a lot of Chinese people eat there so it must be good. Imagine the disappointment of the tourist who sees all the Americans eating at McDonalds and applies the same logic.

Does the fact that I agree with these great minds make me smart? Am I really tapped into the great cosmic wisdom or am I simply looking for validation? What happens when, like with Locke, for everything you agree with that makes you want to stand and shout "Right on!" there's something you can't stand or is just factually wrong?

God bless him, Montaigne addresses that one head on:

> "... this capacity for sifting truth, however much or little of it I may have, and this free will not to enslave my belief easily, I owe principally to myself. For the firmest and most general ideas I have are those which, in a manner of speaking, were born with me. They are naturally and wholly mine. I produced them crude and simple, boldly and strongly, but a little vaguely and imperfectly. Since then I have established and fortified them by the authority of others and the sound argument of the ancients with whom I found my judgment in agreement. These men have given me a firmer grip on my ideas and a fuller enjoyment and possession of them.   —"Of the Force of Imagination"

Let's look at that again in slow motion. What he's really saying is

- We know the rules of the game and what we believe to be true very early on
- As we read we look at what others have said and hold our

thoughts up against them

- When there's a match, it makes our case for us, often finding just the right words to say what we've been trying to spit out for ourselves

Case in point, that's what I've been doing here. Wayne, you're not supposed to swallow everything whole, but sift through and pick the pieces you need.

Let's look at where I am. I have discovered that while many of the people I've read have good points to make, I tend to be more of a Stoic (stuff happens) than an Epicurean (eat drink and be merry because stuff will happen).

As a result, when I stumble over something that rings true in Epictetus or Marcus Aurelius or whatever, it really rings true. When I come across something from another source that contradicts what I think at least I have something to compare it to.

Sometimes I reevaluate my position; usually I look at the two and say, "Nope, I was right in the first place" and move on, but the added advantage is, my belief is that much stronger because the point has been supported.

That is incredibly empowering, if a little scary. You can't take anyone's word for how to run your life or what to believe because if you don't really believe it you will be constantly quoting someone else and ignoring your own mind. The arguments are weak and you get defensive. That's also how people wind up being burned at the stake.

On the other hand, if you really believe it and actively question and process the information, your belief will be stronger and you will be more prone to live in accordance with that belief.

What's amazing about Montaigne isn't the brilliance of his thoughts; although he is certainly smarter than the average bear, it's that he believed those thoughts to be worth writing down in the first place.

Think about it. He was a lawyer and layman, not a theologian or a professional scholar. He was just a guy who had something to say on any number of topics ranging from the education of children to how to be a good friend to somebody and decided to write it for the world to see, making the radical assumption that his opinion was as valid as Plato's or Aquinas' or anyone else.

The essay, or "test" as Montaigne called it, is a common enough form now, but for hundreds of years it was lost. Oh, there was no shortage of treatises and religious material created, but not since the days of Rome or Athens had a lay person written much of anything for the world to see. More to the point, it was written in prose, as opposed to verse, so that the content was more important than the form, and it was easy to read and understand.

It was called a test because that's what you did. You started with an idea, then worked it out and cited enough credible authority (usually in Latin) that it stood the test of logic.

It was a simple concept with a radical core. What was the point of reading and learning if it didn't help you take action? Every individual was worth as much as every other, and if your mind was capable of an original thought, it was as valid as anyone else's. The fact that it agreed with Socrates or Horace or Lucretius merely increased the odds that you were right or that someone might think you were.

While I like a lot of what Montaigne had to say, I am more struck by the sheer audacity of it all: That one man's life would be of sufficient interest to other people that it's worth writing down and that total strangers will want to read it.

Imagine how the world changed as a result. The notion that people with an idea could just—well, just write it for the world to see opened the floodgates. Anyone with an idea could put it out for public consumption. The better the argument, the more likely it would be appreciated.

From Rousseau to Mike Royko, from Susan Sontag to Erma Bombeck.

What about me? What if I wanted to share what I've been uncovering in these old books? Would anyone care? Maybe not, but I at least have permission to try.

Montaigne took the stuff, and sometimes the unpleasant stuff, of every day life and put it out there for the world to see. "Kings and philosophers move their bowels, even women," he says. Okay, we know it's true. Did he have to say that?

Well, yes.

I had to laugh at some of the things he talked about. Interestingly, the church didn't object to even his more atheistic writing, but they did occasionally ask him to tone down the language and eliminate some of the more ummm...unpleasant images.

News flash: Sex and bodily functions are funny. Always have been, always will be for a very simple reason—they get your attention and they hit you where you live.

We may not all quote Horace or Virgil, but we all occasionally have to got to the bathroom, powder our noses,

pinch a loaf,

hang a rat,

see a man about a horse,

siphon the old python,

drain the lizard,

play "sink the cigarette."

Let's face it, for something we're not supposed to talk about we, as a species, have been awfully creative in finding ways to describe it.

I've spent too many years in smoky nightclubs fighting for my survival not to appreciate the power of a good poop joke when the opportunity arises. No, I know Jerry Seinfeld never resorts to bathroom humor. Neither does Bill Cosby. On the other hand, Montaigne did, as did Shakespeare, Epictetus, Homer, Jonathan Swift, Balzac, and Martin Luther.

Not bad company to be in. All I can say is, "Pull my finger."

The issue of transgression and dirty words is as old as writing itself. How do I really feel about it?

In my daily life, I struggle constantly to watch my language. Part of this is the result of having an eight-year-old, who seems determined to copy only the attitudes and behaviors I least like in myself.

Just as importantly, learning to edit myself was an important component in my ability to shift from the stand-up world to the corporate world. I know all too well the advantages and pitfalls of dirty words, as did Montaigne and a surprisingly large number of the classic writers.

Words are one thing, themes are another. I learned early on that people use words writers use as an excuse not to address the themes behind them. They try to throw out Huck Finn from the local library because it uses the "N" word. It's a whole lot easier to do that than acknowledge that's the way their great grandfathers really thought and talked and why a whole lot of our fellow citizens aren't very fond of us.

I look back at the choices I've made in these notes. Even though they're written only for me I notice that I've chosen not to use a lot of the words I thought about. Instead I chose #$%^ or some other way of indicating it without actually saying it.

It's a habit I picked up when I was a kid, reading comic strips. First, it had the feel of the forbidden. Secondly, my fevered Baptist imagination probably filled in those blanks with considerably more vehemence, venom, and creativity than the author even intended. Third, everyone knew what I meant, but I didn't get my mouth washed out with soap.

The notion that the author really felt the need to protect the reader gave me that much more of a sense of naughtiness and power than if I'd actually written—the word itself. There's one more bonus to this method. The writer can make you think the word, use it context, get all the advantages of having used it for the shock value while keeping the moral high ground. The reader has the dirty mind, not me. How cool is that?

I always had the reputation of a "clean" comedian, at least by nightclub standards. I learned a long time ago that the words you used limited the subject matter you could talk about.

Comics who used the "F-word" as a verb, noun, pronoun, adjective, adverb, conjunction, punctuation, and occasionally as a participle (dangling or otherwise) didn't get the point. When called on it, they'd always claim the First Amendment (even the Canadians, who don't have a first amendment, but do apparently have too much American TV) or the performer's right to shock sensibilities. I call it the Lenny Bruce Didn't Die in Vain defense. The problem is that most of the people who use it fail to understand that it was the subject matter, not the words he used, that got Lenny in trouble. That and a small problem finding decent places in which to hide his laudanum.

In the hands of a Pryor or a Carlin the words can be tools, effective ways to make your point, grab people by the verbal lapels and make them listen to what you have to say. In less capable hands it's not far different from your four-year-old saying poopies for the first time and giggling behind their hands.

I'm not some kind of saint here. I am second to no one in my appreciation of a good dirty joke, and profanity in the hands of a master craftsman can be hilarious. I guess the issue is that it's a spice and should be used sparingly and in conjunction with the right ingredients.

Here's my evidence. When some lame comic or movie character swears every ten seconds, I don't notice. When my Baptists Sunday school teacher mother swore traffic stopped.

Now that's power.

Montaigne's essays are an easy read, at least in translation, and very modern in their approach. I can't quite shake the constant references to his right to use the masters of the past to cement his right to his own opinions and that each person's opinion is as valuable as any other, so long as the point is made with authority and style.

Anyone? Is he trying to tell me something?

This is a big chunk of Montaigne's essay on the power of imagination. Among his observations are the point, which every man knows that no matter how sick or hungry you are, you can still want sex. This, by the way, explains overpopulation in countries where there isn't enough food. Although how they get sex without taking the woman to a nice dinner is a mystery to me... I chose this essay mostly because it ties to what happened next in a way that, were I prone to believe in fate, would certainly make me go hmmmmm.

OF THE FORCE OF IMAGINATION
— Michel de Montaigne, 1580

A count of a very great family, and with whom I was very intimate, being married to a fair lady, who had formerly been courted by one who was at the wedding, all his friends were in very great fear; but especially an old lady his kinswoman, who had the ordering of the solemnity, and in whose house it was kept, suspecting his rival would offer foul play by these sorceries. Which fear she communicated to me. I bade her rely upon me: I had, by chance, about me a certain flat plate of gold, whereon were graven some celestial figures, supposed good against sunstroke or pains in the head, being applied to the suture; where, that it might the better remain firm, it was sewed to a ribbon to be tied under the chin; a foppery cousin-german to this of which I am speaking. Jaques Pelletier, who lived in my house, had presented this to me for a singular rarity. I had a fancy to make some use of this knack, and therefore privately told the count, that he might possibly run the same fortune other bridegrooms had sometimes done, especially some one being in the house, who, no doubt, would be glad to do him such a courtesy: but let him boldly go to bed. For I would do him the office of a friend, and, if need were, would not spare a miracle it was in my power to do, provided he would engage to me, upon his honor, to keep it to himself; and only, when they came to bring him his caudle, if matters had not gone well with him, to give me such a sign, and leave the rest to me. Now he had had his ears so battered, and his mind so prepossessed with the eternal tattle of this business, that when he came to't, he did really find himself tied with the trouble of his imagination, and, accordingly, at the time appointed, gave me the sign. Whereupon, I whispered him in the ear, that he should rise, under pretense of putting us out of the room, and after a jesting manner pull my nightgown from my shoulders—we were of much about the same height—throw it over his own, and there keep it till he had performed what I had appointed him to do, which was, that when we were all gone out of the chamber he should withdraw to make water, should three times repeat such and such words, and as often do such and such actions; that at every of the three times, he should tie the ribbon I put into his hand about his middle, and be sure to place the medal that was fastened to it, the figures in such a posture, exactly upon his reins, which being done, and having the last of the three times so well girt and fast tied the ribbon that it could neither untie nor slip from its place, let him confidently return to his business, and withal not forget to spread my gown upon the bed, so that it might be sure to cover them both. These ape's tricks are the main of the effect, our fancy being so far seduced as to believe that such strange means must, of necessity, proceed from some abstruse science: their very inanity gives them weight and reverence. And, certain it is, that my figures approved themselves more venerian than solar, more active than prohibitive. 'Twas a sudden whimsey, mixed with a little curiosity, that made me do a thing so contrary to my nature; for I am an enemy to all subtle and counterfeit actions, and abominate all manner of trickery, though it be for sport, and to an advantage; for though the action may not be vicious in itself, its mode is vicious.

Amasis, king of Egypt, having married Laodice, a very beautiful Greek virgin, though noted for his abilities elsewhere, found himself quite another man with his wife, and could by no means enjoy her; at which he was so enraged, that he threatened to kill her, suspecting her to be a witch. As 'tis usual in things that consist in fancy, she put him upon devotion, and having, accordingly, made his vows to Venus, he found himself divinely restored the very first night after his oblations and sacrifices. Now women are to blame to entertain us with that disdainful coy, and angry countenance, which extinguishes our vigor, as it kindles our desire; which made the daughter-in-law of Pythagoras say, "That the woman who goes to bed to a man, must put off her modesty with her petticoat, and put it on again with the same." The soul of the assailant being disturbed with many several alarms, readily loses the power of performance; and whoever the imagination has once put this trick upon, and confounded with the shame of it (and she never does it but at the first acquaintance, by reason men are then more ardent and eager, and also, at this first account a man gives of himself, he is much more timorous of miscarrying), having made an ill beginning, he enters into such fever and despite at the accident, as are apt to remain and continue with him upon following occasions.

Married people, having all their time before them, ought never to compel or so much as to offer at the feat, if they do not find themselves quite ready; and it is less unseemly to fail of handselling the nuptial sheets, when a man perceives himself full of agitation and trembling, and to await another opportunity at more private and more composed leisure, than to make himself perpetually miserable, for having misbehaved himself and been baffled at the first assault. Till possession be taken, a man that knows himself subject to this infirmity, should leisurely and by degrees make several little trials and light offers, without obstinately attempting, at once, to force an absolute conquest over his own mutinous and indisposed faculties. Such as know their members to be naturally obedient, need take no other care but only to counterplot their fantasies.

The indocile liberty of this member is very remarkable, so importunately unruly in its timidity and impatience, when we do not require it, and so unseasonably disobedient when we stand most in need of it: so imperiously contesting in authority with the will, and with so much haughty obstinacy denying all solicitation, both of hand and mind. And yet, though his rebellion is so universally complained of, and that proof is thence deduced to condemn him, if he had, nevertheless, feed me to plead his cause, I should, peradventure, bring the rest of his fellow-members into suspicion of complotting this mischief against him, out of pure envy at the importance and pleasure especial to his employment; and to have, by confederacy, armed the whole world against him, by malevolently charging him alone, with their common offense. For let any one consider, whether there is any one part of our bodies that does not often refuse to perform its office at the precept of the will, and that does not often exercise its function in defiance of her command. They have every one of them passions of their own, that rouse and awaken, stupefy and benumb them, without our leave or consent. How often do the involuntary motions of the countenance discover our inward thoughts, and betray our most private secrets to the bystanders. The same cause that animates this member does also, without our knowledge, animate the lungs, pulse, and heart, the sight of a pleasing object imperceptibly diffusing a flame through all our parts, with a feverish motion. Is there nothing but these veins and muscles that swell and flag without the consent, not only of the will, but even of our knowledge also? We do not command our hairs to stand on end, nor our skin to shiver either with fear or desire; the hands often convey themselves to parts to which we do not direct them; the tongue will be interdict, and the voice congealed, when we know not how to help it. When we have nothing to eat, and would willingly forbid it, the appetite does not, for all that, forbear to stir up the parts that are subject to it, no more nor less than the other appetite we were speaking of, and in, like manner, as unseasonably leaves us, when it thinks fit. The vessels that serve to discharge the belly have their own proper dilatations and compressions, without and beyond our concurrence, as well as those which are destined to purge the reins; and that which, to justify the prerogative of the will, St. Augustine urges, of having seen a man who could command his rear to discharge as often together as he pleased, Vives, his commentator, yet further fortifies with another example in his time, of one that could break wind in tune; but these cases do not suppose any more pure obedience in that part; for is anything commonly more tumultuary or indiscreet? To which let me add, that I myself knew one so rude and ungoverned, as for forty years together made his master vent with one continued and unintermitted outbursting, and 'tis like will do so till he die of it. And I could heartily wish that I only knew by reading how often a man's belly, by the denial of one single puff, brings him to the very door of an exceeding painful death; and that the emperor, who gave liberty to let fly in all places, had at the same time given us power to do it. But for our will, in whose behalf we prefer this accusation, with how much greater probability may we reproach herself with mutiny and sedition, for her irregularity and disobedience? Does she always will what we would have her to do? Does she not often will what we forbid her to will, and that to our manifest prejudice? Does she suffer herself, more than any of the rest, to be governed and directed by the results of our reason? To conclude, I should move, in the behalf of the gentleman, my client, it might be considered, that in this fact, his cause being inseparably and indistinctly conjoined with an accessory, yet he only is called in question, and that by arguments and accusations which cannot be charged upon the other; whose business, indeed, it is sometimes inopportunely to invite, but never to refuse, and invite, moreover, after a tacit and quiet manner; and therefore is the malice and injustice of his accusers most manifestly apparent. But be it how it will, protesting against the proceedings of the advocates and judges, Nature will, in the meantime, proceed after her own way, who had done but well had she endowed this member with some particular privilege; the author of the sole immortal work of mortals; a divine work, according to Socrates; and love, the desire of immortality, and himself an immortal demon......

I am solicited to write the affairs of my own time, by some who fancy I look upon them with an eye less blinded with passion than another, and have a clearer insight into them by reason of the free access fortune has given me to the heads of various factions; but they do not consider, that to purchase the glory of Sallust, I would not give myself the trouble, sworn enemy as I am to obligation, assiduity, or perseverance; that there is nothing so contrary to my style as a continued narrative, I so often interrupt, and cut myself short in my writing for want of breath; I have neither composition nor explanation worth anything, and am ignorant, beyond a child, of the phrases and even the very words proper to express the most common things; and for that reason it is, that I have undertaken to say only what I can say, and have accommodated my subject to my strength: should I take one to be my guide, peradventure I should not be able to keep pace with him; and in the freedom of my liberty, might deliver judgments, which upon better thoughts, and according to reason, would be illegitimate and punishable. Plutarch would tell us, of what he has delivered to us, that it is the work of others: that his examples are all and everywhere exactly true: that they are useful to posterity, and are presented with a luster that will light us the way to virtue, is his own work. It is not of so dangerous consequence, as in a medicinal drug, whether an old story be so or no.

FOURTEEN

Interlude #2

Green Tea and Sympathy

I met her at a local bookstore on the kind of day that was so wet and cold you want to contact the ghost of Father Marquette just so you can grab him by the cassock, slap him around a bit and shout, "What kind of stupid place is this to put a city?" What kind of idiot moves *to* Chicago? Oh, never mind.

Betty—her name was—sat at the next table next to the most pathetic looking fichus tree I have ever seen. Its terra cotta pot had something written on it that may have been the house plant equivalent of "Do Not Resuscitate." She was attempting to dry out, her umbrella leaking all over the tiles, a pot of tea in front of her and dressed in Scottish wool with some kind of macramé beret that was completely impractical for the weather.

Her eyes caught me before I even sat down. I know the look; I've seen it a lot since I've moved here. It's the look of someone who might actually be other than a Republican in DuPage county and has spotted a kindred spirit. We aren't many, and frankly we blend in reasonably well for the most part. I think it's the political equivalent of the "gay-dar" that lets my gay friends scan a room and know instantly (and with amazing accuracy) who plays on their team.

I have just escaped The Duchess and Her Serene Highness for an hour and don't really feel much like company. I give her my best "we both know you're crazy so back away now and I won't scream" look. It doesn't work.

Note to self: Practice that one, it's letting you down a lot lately.

"Whatcha writing?"

"It's sort of a book report."

She appraises me for a moment, maybe working out why a forty-year-old schlub would have the same homework as a nine-year-old, but if it bothered her it sure didn't scare her off.

"What's the book?"

I flip it over in my hand, showing it off. "Some essays by Montaigne." It's actually pretty cool how I've gotten better at telling people what I'm reading, making it sound like it's the kind of stuff I read all the time—and gosh, doesn't everybody?

"I've never read him." I shrug a little smugly. "But you know who was crazy about Montaigne?"

I steel myself, thinking that she's either going to tell me it's her crazy ex-husband-who-never-understood-her-needs-and-needs-to-get-in-touch-with-his-inner-child[57] or the pilot of the mother ship who has her love child kept hostage in a mason jar.

"Emerson," she says without a hint of lunacy in her eyes.

I sip my tea and say nothing, surprised for two reasons:

1. it's a far more lucid answer than I expected and;
2. in a plastic bag at my feet is the next book on my list, *Poems and Essays of Ralph Waldo Emerson.*

"He wrote a whole essay about how Montaigne is his hero, and how everybody should be a writer because of him."

"You've read Emerson?"

---

57. An all too common theme with women I meet for the first time. For some reason they feel empowered to share with me the deepest darkest secrets of their soul within the first four minutes. Please remember, unless you have actually bonded, "How are you" is just a polite thing to say, not a probing question.

"Hasn't everyone—in college, I mean?"

"Well, no, but it is on the list." I look down at the book. I swear it just stuck its tongue out at me.

"How could you not have read Emerson? I thought they made everyone read him?"

I resort to my standard excuse for not doing anything people thought I should have as a youth: "I'm Canadian."

"Oh, I didn't know," she says a little embarrassed.

Yeah, it's amazing how well we can blend into normal society. God bless Americans, all you have to do is tell them you were born somewhere else and they'll forgive you darned near anything. It's almost as if since you had the poor judgment to be birthed elsewhere, you're capable of almost any foolishness, you poor thing.

"I love Emerson," she offers… why is that suddenly sexy?

I ask her why. What does Emerson have to offer that's so important? She perks right up and tells me about his faith that individuals know the right things to do, even if they don't always do them; how he could see past the narrowness of nineteenth century New England to a future that included just about everybody. She loved how he believed that everyone was capable of enlightenment if they really wanted it, and that the answers didn't lie in the deep dark past. She is becoming more and more excited as she speaks.

"What's wrong with the past?" I ask, only semi-innocently.

She shakes her head and the soggy wool beret falls onto the table. "Nothing, except you can't live by what somebody said a thousand years ago. You have to use that as a starting point to go forward."

"That's what Montaigne said too."

"Yup. That's why Emerson loved the guy. So is this for school or something?"

"No, just a little project of mine."

"Are you writing a book?"

"Not that I'm aware of." I take a big sip out of my cup. Damn, I hate lukewarm tea. I look up again, and she's still looking at me like she doesn't know whether to believe me or not. She's not going anywhere, apparently.

"Okay, fair's fair. What are you reading?"

She flashes me a thick purple trade paperback. Proust. "Remembrance of Things Past." I'm impressed. I wouldn't tackle that one without oxygen tanks and a Sherpa guide. The Duchess claims to have read it and forgotten what it was about, which is good for extra irony points as far as I'm concerned.

"It must be dead French guy day." I can't resist a gentle poke, just to see what she'll do. "Do you like Dead White Males?"

"Well, I'm partial to live ones, but they'll do in a pinch". She looks away suddenly after shooting me a smile that says "You have officially been flirted with."

Was that an honest-to-God blush I just felt? We're both too old and way too out of practice for this, no matter how innocent it is. "So why Proust?"

"Because I said I would someday—just to prove I could."

That sounds familiar. Another person my age going back to take a run at going forward. How many of us were there? It was becoming some kind of club or something.

"It's slow reading, but not as tough as I thought it would be."

I tip my Cubs cap playfully. "You're a better man than I, Gunga din."

"Kipling, right?"

Not bad lady. I take another look at her. Under all that damp wool she's actually attractive, but I convince myself at least momentarily I'm just dazzled by her knowledge of books.

She leans forward a bit, conspiratorially. "You said he's on your list, which implies there is a list. What's it for?"

I tell her about my little journal project and how I'm finding it more fun than I expected to. She demands to know what's on the list so far.

I flip open my journal and do a quick review and I'm more than a

little surprised by how much its grown in only a couple of months. As I
rattle off a title, she says, "Check" or "Nope."

After a while we're like kids comparing baseball cards; sort of a
need him, need him, got him thing. I pull ahead because I have a
complete set of Russians: Tolstoy to Dostoyevsky to Sholokhov. I'm
feeling magnanimous so I offer to give her bonus points for Proust, but
she says it's a straight-up trade for *War and Peace*.

She asks me point blank, "Okay, so what's worth reading?"

I give her the latest list:

Worth reading	**Glad I did it, but if I do it again there'd better be money involved...**
Plutarch	
Epictetus	
Browning	Horace
Bacon	Cicero
Homer	Milton
Montaigne	Locke
Thackeray	Erasmus
Balzac	Lucretius

I confess that leaves me with one book that I don't know which
category it belongs in. I feel about *Robinson Crusoe* the way I feel about
Deuce Bigelow, Male Gigolo. I liked it a lot but I'm more than a little
wary of recommending it to anyone else.

She laughs, a little snorting thing. "Is that in your journal?"

"It bloody well is now," I promise myself.

"You should write a book," she pronounces in that tone total
strangers use when giving you life-altering advice. "I'd buy it, just so I
could know what books were worth reading. I mean, I can't get to them
all."

Somehow the fact that I'll never get to them all hadn't occurred to me until that very moment, and I found it more than a little unsettling. "Yeah, like anybody cares what I think," I say lightly.

She has begun to put her belongings into her oh-so-politically-correct mesh bag and stops cold. She gives me a puzzled look for a moment and says, "You have soooooo got to read Emerson." And she's up and gone.

I take my last mouthful of tea, by now it's almost as cold and just plain nasty as the weather outside, but it doesn't put a damper on the afternoon. It was fun talking to another bibliophile, and it has been a long time since a sober woman actively flirted with me, so long ago that I almost didn't recognize when it happened.

And she said she'd read a book if someone like me wrote one. Of course the key words there are "someone like" but still ... the idea is appealing and it's been nibbling around the edges of my brain for a couple of weeks now.

Then there was the whole Emerson connection. That was a pretty freaky coincidence, I think as I pack up my things to brave the elements. I wonder why she was so set on my reading Emerson?

FIFTEEN

With Just a Little More Help I Can Be Self-Reliant

Ralph Waldo Emerson

> Books are the best of things, well used; abused, among the worst. What is the right use? What is the one end which all means go to effect? They are for nothing but to inspire. I had better never see a book than to be warped by it out of my own orbit and made a satellite instead of a system.
>
> —Ralph Waldo Emerson, "The American Scholar," 1837

Since I started keeping this journal, two things have nagged at me. The first is how whatever I'm reading at the moment, no matter how old or obscure, seems to resonate with what's going on in my life. The second is what I'm supposed to do with this journal, since my shelf of Classics Clubs is almost empty.

I didn't have any expectations for Emerson, not knowing much about him except for the odd quote. Starting with that weird conversation in the bookstore yesterday, though, he seems to be popping up everywhere.

The first essay in this book is "The American Scholar," and what is Emerson talking about but the role that reading the works of the past should have on a reader. I have just finished reading Cicero, Locke, and Bacon. So what do I find on page 8:

> "Meek men grow up in libraries, believing it their duty to accept the views which Cicero, which Locke, which Bacon have given; forgetful that Cicero, Locke and Bacon were only young men in libraries when they wrote these books.

In other words, they put their intellectual pants on one leg at a time, same as you and I do.

Our duty then is to use these books for their intended purpose; not to tell us what to do and enslave us, but to inspire us. He writes that we are not supposed to do nothing but read—that's wasted time: "When he can read God directly, the hour is too precious to be wasted in other men's transcripts of their readings". But when we are uninspired, or feel cut off, we read and should be inspired to action again: "We hear that we may speak."

Lord knows I've been feeling uninspired and cut off. Well, I was when I started this project at any rate. I'm not nearly feeling that way as strongly now. Is this what the woman in the bookstore was talking about? How could she have known that was what I needed to hear right now? I have never been a believer in omens or cosmic coincidence, but this is almost creepy.

To open a book and stumble into something like it's meant for me is weird enough, but Emerson goes even further.

Later he talks about reading Montaigne and getting the strange feeling that whatever he's reading at the moment relates to whatever project he's working on. Not since my first Penthouse Letter have I read something that connected so immediately to where my current obsessions lay.

I need to think about this for a while.

Flipping back through these journal pages, I keep finding references to nuggets or pearls that I find even among the obnoxious or obsolete stuff that needs to be thrown out like yesterday's tuna melt. Not surprisingly, there's a line for that too, "The discerning will read, in his Plato or Shakespeare, only that least part—only the authentic utterances of the oracle; all the rest he rejects, were it never so many times Plato's and Shakespeare's."

That's it. That's precisely what I started doing; at first unconciously and then purposely sifting through works of the past to uncover those pearls that I really need when I really need them.

I have always done that. I remember when I was thirteen, uncovering a great piece of wisdom in a trash novel. *The Executioner* was a series of cheap paperbacks about a Vietnam vet who comes home and declares war on the Mafia. Besides personally exterminating everyone in America whose name ended in the letter *i*, Mack Bolan taught a fifteen-year-old boy a valuable lesson….

"Once is happenstance, twice is coincidence, and three times is enemy action". That simple lesson—not to jump to conclusions but act when they're confirmed—has been a cornerstone of my professional life. If I can draw value from a dime-store novel, surely I can find something of value in works by writers superior to Don Pendleton, assuming such a person exists.

More essays, more epiphanies. For the last few months I've been reading and thinking about a lot of subjects by a lot of writers I never thought I was fit to read, never mind emulate. All this time I wasn't performing amazing feats of mental derring-do, I was merely recharging my batteries and confirming that I am on the right path.

I know what to do.

I know when I'm right.

I know what to do when I'm not.

So do it, Monkey Boy. You're out of excuses.

I discover his "Divinity School Address" and it seems to mirror almost exactly my feeling towards religion. I actually shout "Yes!" while reading it. Emerson's belief that there is a universal goodness, that there is so much to love and admire in the words of Jesus—beyond all other prophets—and yet there is so much harm and evil done in his name rings true.

It's why even as I become more actively spiritual than at any time in my life, I am still reluctant to tie myself to a particular church. In the end, they're all partly right, and all equally off the mark. But maybe most importantly, I know what's worth keeping and what's to be ignored where it can be.

I pray now, at least more often than I ever have. Not in the way I used to, like the Big Daddy in the sky will give me something if I'm good. My prayers now are for understanding, and consist more of listening than talking. forty years it took me to learn how to shut up and I still need the occasional reminder.

Reading his essay, "Self-Reliance" I can almost feel Emerson grab me by the lapels and shake me. I don't need to live in the heart of the city, or travel to Europe,—the suburbs are fine. I don't need to be adored by more than The Duchess and Her Serene Highness—people who already adore me more than I deserve. I don't need more money— well, okay but only a little more and I don't need it to be happier, just more comfortable and they're not the same thing. Epictetus said the same thing, of course, but somehow it doesn't strike me as powerfully. Maybe he was just softening me up for Emerson.

Essay after essay, the points are finding their marks like darts in a bullseye. In forty years I can't remember reading anything that has had this effect on me. And what is it he's saying? Nothing I didn't already know. Nothing I haven't gleaned from a lifetime of experiences and wisdom passed down through books, wall plaques, and coffee mugs. It's all so obvious. So why is it such a big deal?

Somehow in turning forty and dealing with the lunacy that is work, the skewing of priorities and the focus on things I can't control—I had forgotten what I knew. Like Emerson, and Montaigne before him, I just needed to confirm it by checking with the authorities before moving on.

In a wonderful biography of Emerson, *Mind On Fire*,[58] I learn that his sources are mine, that he adored Montaigne and kept Epictetus and Marcus Aurelius near his bed for inspiration (and proved in the process you can be a Stoic and not be a conservative, which is perhaps the single most comforting thing I can take out of his biography).

I can't fight the feeling that this project is almost over, that I've done whatever it is I'm supposed to do with it. I have a couple of more books on my shelf to go and I will complete this task (if only to say I did). Then what?

Okay, I'm finally asking the question out loud: Is there a book buried in all these notes? I would love there to be. I used to think there was no way, that I have nothing to say that hasn't been said before, and far better. Now I'm not so sure.

I know there are people out there asking questions just as I am, and looking in the same places. My anonymous cardiologist friend on the plane, Betty the bookstore apparition, friends and acquaintances have heard what I'm doing with my journal and responded with enthusiasm and tons of questions.

Do they care what I have to say?

Do I care if they care?

This section from "The American Scholar", of all the pieces I read to create this journal just struck like a slap to the back of the head. That it goaded me into trying to turn this into a book may be thought of as a mixed blessing, I grant you.

---

58. This is a great book by Robert D. Richardson Jr. Hey, let's give credit where it's due. I don't need to get all Stephen Ambrose about this.

THE AMERICAN SCHOLAR
— Ralph Waldo Emerson, 1837

II. The next great influence into the spirit of the scholar, is, the mind of the Past, — in whatever form, whether of literature, of art, of institutions, that mind is inscribed. Books are the best type of the influence of the past, and perhaps we shall get at the truth, — learn the amount of this influence more conveniently, — by considering their value alone.

The theory of books is noble. The scholar of the first age received into him the world around; brooded thereon; gave it the new arrangement of his own mind, and uttered it again. It came into him, life; it went out from him, truth. It came to him, short-lived actions; it went out from him, immortal thoughts. It came to him, business; it went from him, poetry. It was dead fact; now, it is quick thought. It can stand, and it can go. It now endures, it now flies, it now inspires. Precisely in proportion to the depth of mind from which it issued, so high does it soar, so long does it sing.

Or, I might say, it depends on how far the process had gone, of transmuting life into truth. In proportion to the completeness of the distillation, so will the purity and imperishableness of the product be. But none is quite perfect. As no air-pump can by any means make a perfect vacuum, so neither can any artist entirely exclude the conventional, the local, the perishable from his book, or write a book of pure thought, that shall be as efficient, in all respects, to a remote posterity, as to cotemporaries, or rather to the second age. Each age, it is found, must write its own books; or rather, each generation for the next succeeding. The books of an older period will not fit this.

Yet hence arises a grave mischief. The sacredness which attaches to the act of creation, — the act of thought, — is transferred to the record. The poet chanting, was felt to be a divine man: henceforth the chant is divine also. The writer was a just and wise spirit: henceforward it is settled, the book is perfect; as love of the hero corrupts into worship of his statue. Instantly, the book becomes noxious: the guide is a tyrant. The sluggish and perverted mind of the multitude, slow to open to the incursions of Reason, having once so opened, having once received this book, stands upon it, and makes an outcry, if it is disparaged. Colleges are built on it. Books are written on it by thinkers, not by Man Thinking; by men of talent, that is, who start wrong, who set out from accepted dogmas, not from their own sight of principles. Meek young men grow up in libraries, believing it their duty to accept the views, which Cicero, which Locke, which Bacon, have given, forgetful that Cicero, Locke, and Bacon were only young men in libraries, when they wrote these books.

Hence, instead of Man Thinking, we have the bookworm. Hence, the book-learned class, who value books, as such; not as related to nature and the human constitution, but as making a sort of Third Estate with the world and the soul. Hence, the restorers of readings, the emendators, the bibliomaniacs of all degrees.

Books are the best of things, well used; abused, among the worst. What is the right use? What is the one end, which all means go to effect? They are for nothing but to inspire. I had better never see a book, than to be warped by its attraction clean out of my own orbit, and made a satellite instead of a system. The one thing in the world, of value, is the active soul. This every man is entitled to; this every man contains within him, although, in almost all men, obstructed, and as yet unborn. The soul active sees absolute truth; and utters truth, or creates. In this action, it is genius; not the privilege of here and there a favorite, but the sound estate of every man. In its essence, it is progressive.

The book, the college, the school of art, the institution of any kind, stop with some past utterance of genius. This is good, say they, — let us hold by this. They pin me down. They look backward and not forward. But genius looks forward: the eyes of man are set in his forehead, not in his hindhead: man hopes:

genius creates. Whatever talents may be, if the man create not, the pure efflux of the Deity is not his; — cinders and smoke there may be, but not yet flame. There are creative manners, there are creative actions, and creative words; manners, actions, words, that is, indicative of no custom or authority, but springing spontaneous from the mind's own sense of good and fair.

On the other part, instead of being its own seer, let it receive from another mind its truth, though it were in torrents of light, without periods of solitude, inquest, and self-recovery, and a fatal disservice is done. Genius is always sufficiently the enemy of genius by over influence. The literature of every nation bear me witness. The English dramatic poets have Shakspearized now for two hundred years.

Undoubtedly there is a right way of reading, so it be sternly subordinated. Man Thinking must not be subdued by his instruments. Books are for the scholar's idle times. When he can read God directly, the hour is too precious to be wasted in other men's transcripts of their readings. But when the intervals of darkness come, as come they must, — when the sun is hid, and the stars withdraw their shining, — we repair to the lamps which were kindled by their ray, to guide our steps to the East again, where the dawn is. We hear, that we may speak. The Arabian proverb says, "A fig tree, looking on a fig tree, becometh fruitful."

It is remarkable, the character of the pleasure we derive from the best books. They impress us with the conviction, that one nature wrote and the same reads. We read the verses of one of the great English poets, of Chaucer, of Marvell, of Dryden, with the most modern joy, — with a pleasure, I mean, which is in great part caused by the abstraction of all *time* from their verses. There is some awe mixed with the joy of our surprise, when this poet, who lived in some past world, two or three hundred years ago, says that which lies close to my own soul, that which I also had wellnigh thought and said. But for the evidence thence afforded to the philosophical doctrine of the identity of all minds, we should suppose some preestablished harmony, some

foresight of souls that were to be, and some preparation of
stores for their future wants, like the fact observed in insects,
who lay up food before death for the young grub they shall never
see.

I would not be hurried by any love of system, by any
exaggeration of instincts, to underrate the Book. We all know,
that, as the human body can be nourished on any food, though it
were boiled grass and the broth of shoes, so the human mind
can be fed by any knowledge. And great and heroic men have
existed, who had almost no other information than by the
printed page. I only would say, that it needs a strong head to
bear that diet. One must be an inventor to read well. As the
proverb says, "He that would bring home the wealth of the
Indies, must carry out the wealth of the Indies." There is then
creative reading as well as creative writing. When the mind is
braced by labor and invention, the page of whatever book we
read becomes luminous with manifold allusion. Every sentence is
doubly significant, and the sense of our author is as broad as the
world. We then see, what is always true, that, as the seer's hour
of vision is short and rare among heavy days and months, so is
its record, perchance, the least part of his volume. The
discerning will read, in his Plato or Shakespeare, only that least
part, — only the authentic utterances of the oracle; — all the rest
he rejects, were it never so many times Plato's and
Shakespeare's.

Of course, there is a portion of reading quite indispensable
to a wise man. History and exact science he must learn by
laborious reading. Colleges, in like manner, have their
indispensable office, — to teach elements. But they can only
highly serve us, when they aim not to drill, but to create; when
they gather from far every ray of various genius to their
hospitable halls, and, by the concentrated fires, set the hearts of
their youth on flame. Thought and knowledge are natures in
which apparatus and pretension avail nothing. Gowns, and
pecuniary foundations, though of towns of gold, can never

countervail the least sentence or syllable of wit. Forget this, and our American colleges will recede in their public importance, whilst they grow richer every year.

SIXTEEN

"One Fish Two Fish" for Grown-Ups

Lucretius, "On the Nature of Things"

> Yet there be who, blind to all the ways
> Of matter, cling perversely to the creed
> That not without a power divine do ways
> So nicely tempered to the needs of man
> Could Nature bring her changing seasons round
> And rouse to bring the crops and all beside
> Which goodly Pleasure, guide of life, doth tempt
> Mankind to approach, and with her kindly hand
> Still leading on, doth leave them with the arts
> Of love their generations to renew,
> Lest humankind should perish from the earth.
> — Lucretius, *On the Nature of Things,*
> (translated by Charles E. Bennet)

This is another one of those books that falls under the heading of glad I did it, but don't EVER ask me to go through that again.

Imagine if you will, the longest, most out of date science text book you ever had thrust upon you, only now it's in the form of a poem that goes on for 300 pages. That's essentially what *On the Nature of Things* is. While I stand in awe of the degree of difficulty involved, I'd rather

176

bludgeon myself with a sack of wolverines than go through that again.

And to be completely fair to Lucretius, it's not all his fault, nor is there nothing here worth reading. There are two major problems this reasonably intelligent man has with the book:

1. the science is just plain wrong so much of the time that it's difficult to appreciate and;
2. Lucretius is an Epicurean, which means he believes in no higher power or force beyond the atomic.

While the sections of the book that deal with the spiritual realm are well written and even mildly funny at times, they don't ring true to me. Again, with anyone reading these books the question arises, "Can you appreciate work that you fundamentally disagree with?"

Epicureans tend to be the bad boys of classical philosophy. They mostly were responding to the Greek and Roman religions which were full of ceremony and stories of the gods that seemed patently ridiculous, so they began to focus on the observable and the scientific. Hmmmmmm, no relevance there at all.

Everything, they claimed, came down to atoms. No Divine Power, no capricious gods with deep-seated emotional problems, no need to confuse the issue with superstition and empty ritual. From there it became a small step to the "eat, drink, and be merry" attitude that has come to be synonymous with Epicureans.[59]

More than the Stoic "stuff happens," the Epicureans believed that "stuff happens, it's all according to the laws of physics (rather than some mystic plan we don't understand) and there's absolutely nothing you can do about it so let's party like it's A.D. 99."

I agree with the shots at religious superstition. Whether it's sacrificing a goat to Apollo or crossing yourself before you go to bat, these are frequently empty gestures designed to appease some deity with a bad attitude and they don't hold much water, regardless of how

---

59. Epicure magazine, for example, is long on artery-choking recipes and a bit light on philosophy. Not a bad thing, just an observation.

fervently they're done.

My mother used to say, "going to church doesn't make you a Christian any more than sitting in the garage makes you an Oldsmobile." She came from the wall-plaque and cute sayings school of theology, but she had a point. That stuff is window dressing, and if it doesn't touch you at a much deeper level it doesn't mean a whole lot.

That deeper level becomes the issue for me, and where I part company with Lucretius and the philosophical equivalent of the Rat Pack, is what that level consists of. To hear him tell it, we experience physical and chemical reactions to stimuli that we *interpret* as being more than they really are.

I'm not buying it. I suppose as a younger man I did (it justifies all kinds of behavior from dodging Sunday school to sleeping with your roommate's girlfriend)[60] but no more. Maybe my desire to connect with my immortal soul is directly related to how much closer I am to shuffling it off than I used to be. But I do have a soul that is more than an atomic processor.

Even Lucretius, as much of an Epicure as he was, struggled with this one. He believed there was an "anima" which is thought, and "animus" which is the life force. To my mind, those are two totally different levels. To Lucretius, they were different ways of processing the same information.

Inspired by my reading, though, let me take a run at formulating an argument:

- Throughout history, human beings have tried to attain reconciliation with something we'll call the life force (or the divine, or whatever)
- Like spleens, appendixes, and other vestigial organs there is a purpose for that, even if we don't know exactly what it is

---

60. I've checked: The statute of limitations is up on that behavior and besides none of them know which roommate I'm talking about. Let them sweat it out—half of them still owe me for phone bills.

- Therefore, there must be something that appeases that desire and satisfies the spiritual quest that's such a big part of being human

That little theory probably wouldn't even earn me a passing grade in a philosophy class, but since it's my first attempt, I kind of like it. At least it touches on why I can't totally reject the notion of spirituality, even with my major reservations about religion as such.

So I'm back in church after twenty years. It all started when my daughter was new born. I was in Toronto performing and staying with a friend. On a whim, I went to an old Anglican church to hear the music they were playing for Good Friday.

Sitting in that Toronto church, listening to Faure's Requiem, I felt an electric connection to something higher that was more than a physical reaction to neurons firing in mathematical patterns.

There is a Good, a True, and a Beautiful and as a species we've spent our entire evolution trying to tap into it. There are a million names for it, but the characteristics are remarkably similar. Like the Epicureans, most of us have at one time or another felt revulsion at the excesses and occasional silliness of capital-R Religion.

Unlike them, a lot of us believe that what we have there is a breakdown in process, not a rejection of the basic theory. The problem is that you can't observe the spiritual realm using tools designed for measuring the physical. Those who reject the notion of a spirit or a divine just aren't using the right observation tools.

Let me use a really basic example. You can read about skiing. You can watch the Olympics. You can talk to people who do it and appreciate that they feel something unique about the experience, but you haven't skied until you have strapped the boards to your feet, defied gravity and prepared to straddle a pine tree at thirty miles an hour.[61]

You can know that there is such a thing as cold, that people feel a certain way about it, that it's a physical sensation, but until you've slept

---

61. Ken Wilber explains this much more eloquently than I do in several books. Start with *A Theory of Everything*.

with my wife's feet on your back, you don't know what cold is.

It's logical then, that you can't really pass judgment on the spiritual unless you've done things that actually touch the spiritual—you have to *do* something. It's picking the something that works for you that gives people fits. My feeble but well-intentioned attempts at meditation are part of that.

One reason I've decided to work with the Dead White Guys is that they're familiar and to follow their advice I don't have to do anything too outside my own pillowy soft Western experience. I can understand, and even attempt on occasion, kneeling in prayer, fasting, giving up something for Lent and even Gregorian Chant (which I've started listening to in my office when I have to crank out another mindless project update). On the other hand, twisting myself into a pretzel, chanting in Urdu, and permanent vegetarianism aren't going to cut it.

His definition of what happens to you when you die is equally uninspiring. He talks about the spirit or life force being made of smaller atoms (seed, he calls them) than the surrounding flesh. When you die the seeds simply dissolve and disappear through the skin into the air. Gone, kaput, no more.

It's an easy conclusion to draw if you're only using your physical senses. I have only seen death up close once (God, do I really want to talk about this?) and it looked a little like that.

I have only been present at the moment of one death—my mother's. Drained from a seven-year battle with cancer, she's lying in a hospital bed, drawn, ashen, breathing through a tube and in a morphine coma; she may as well be dead—but she's not. There is something still there.

Then there isn't. No spasm of release. She didn't so much let out a last gasp as just never take in another breath, but I knew the second she was dead. Something that had been there only an eye blink before was suddenly not there any more, and my father and I both knew it. What was left was a whole lot of atoms and things, but it wasn't Walline.

Did the small seeds of her soul simply escape the shell of her body?

Seems as logical an explanation as any at a time when *what* happened didn't seem nearly as important as the *why*.

Since he's an Epicurean, life and death are simply phenomenae to be examined, nothing to worry about so besides death, he talks about the facts of life in a pretty unvarnished manner.

Again, just to prove my Philistinism has no depth to which it won't sink, even when discussing the implications of an immortal soul I'm still giggling over the dirty parts—sheesh.

Since he's talking about nature, it makes sense that Lucretius would refer to the stuff of reproduction, but there's something disconcerting about 2000-year-old references to wet dreams, faked orgasms, and low sperm count.[62]

Would I read Lucretius again? Probably not. It's a tough read even in a fairly modern translation, and the science is exposed and laughable to us now. Still, you have to admire someone who has the cajones to write the definitive work of his time on physics, chemistry and biology—and do it all in rhyme no less.

Just imagine Stephen Hawking attempting the same feat:

> There once was a very black hole
> To swallow the world was its goal
> It ate like a shark
> Till nary a quark
> Escaped and it swallowed us whole

Try 300-plus pages of THAT.

Okay, so you think physics was a bear in high school. Try deciphering this one. It's Lucretius attempting to explain that the universe is boundless. It's actually a pretty cool argument, not unlike the "thought experiments" Einstein did to explain relativity. Truth is, I don't know if it makes sense or not, but it sounds good and shut up a lot of the naysayers, which I suspect was the whole point in the first place.

---

62. It's in book four, the last 500 or so verses—and shame on you.

THE NATURE OF THINGS, "BOOK 2"
— Titus Lucretius Carus 50 B.C.E
(translation by William Ellery Leonard)

Thus, then, the All that is is limited
In no one region of its onward paths,
For then 'tmust have forever its beyond.
And a beyond 'tis seen can never be
For aught, unless still further on there be
A somewhat somewhere that may bound the same—
So that the thing be seen still on to where
The nature of sensation of that thing
Can follow it no longer. Now because
Confess we must there's naught beside the sum,
There's no beyond, and so it lacks all end.
It matters nothing where thou post thyself,
In whatsoever regions of the same;
Even any place a man has set him down
Still leaves about him the unbounded all
Outward in all directions; or, supposing
moment the all of space finite to be,
If some one farthest traveller runs forth
Unto the extreme coasts and throws ahead
A flying spear, is't then thy wish to think
It goes, hurled off amain, to where 'twas sent
And shoots afar, or that some object there
Can thwart and stop it? For the one or other
Thou must admit; and take. Either of which
Shuts off escape for thee, and does compel
That thou concede the all spreads everywhere,
Owning no confines. Since whether there be
Aught that may block and check it so it comes
Not where 'twas sent, nor lodges in its goal,
Or whether borne along, in either view

'Thas started not from any end. And so
I'll follow on, and whereso'er thou set
The extreme coasts, I'll query, "what becomes
Thereafter of thy spear?" 'Twill come to pass
That nowhere can a world's-end be, and that
The chance for further flight prolongs forever
The flight itself. Besides, were all the space
Of the totality and sum shut in
With fixed coasts, and bounded everywhere,
Then would the abundance of world's matter flow
Together by solid weight from everywhere
Still downward to the bottom of the world,
Nor aught could happen under cope of sky,
Nor could there be a sky at all or sun—
Indeed, where matter all one heap would lie,
By having settled during infinite time.
But in reality, repose is given
Unto no bodies 'mongst the elements,
Because there is no bottom whereunto
They might, as 'twere, together flow, and where
They might take up their undisturbed abodes.
In endless motion everything goes on
Forevermore; out of all regions, even
Out of the pit below, from forth the vast,
Are hurtled bodies evermore supplied.
The nature of room, the space of the abyss
Is such that even the flashing thunderbolts
Can neither speed upon their courses through,
Gliding across eternal tracts of time,
Nor, further, bring to pass, as on they run,
That they may bate their journeying one whit:
Such huge abundance spreads for things around—
Room off to every quarter, without end.
Lastly, before our very eyes is seen
Thing to bound thing: air hedges hill from hill,
And mountain walls hedge air; land ends the sea,

And sea in turn all lands; but for the All
Truly is nothing which outside may bound.
That, too, the sum of things itself may not
Have power to fix a measure of its own,
Great Nature guards, she who compels the void
To bound all body, as body all the void,
Thus rendering by these alternates the whole
An infinite; or else the one or other,
Being unbounded by the other, spreads,
Even by its single nature, ne'ertheless
Immeasurably forth....
Nor sea, nor earth, nor shining vaults of sky,
Nor breed of mortals, nor holy limbs of gods
Could keep their place least portion of an hour:
For, driven apart from out its meetings fit,
The stock of stuff, dissolved, would be borne
Along the illimitable inane afar,
Or rather, in fact, would never have once combined
And given a birth to aught, since, scattered wide,
It could not be united. For of truth
Neither by counsel did the primal germs
'Stablish themselves, as by keen act of mind,
Each in its proper place; nor did they make,
Forsooth, a compact how each germ should move;
But since, being many and changed in many modes
Along the All, they're driven abroad and vexed
By blow on blow, even from all time of old,
They thus at last, after attempting all
The kinds of motion and conjoining, come
Into those great arrangements out of which
This sum of things established is create,
By which, moreover, through the mighty years,
It is preserved, when once it has been thrown
Into the proper motions, bringing to pass
That ever the streams refresh the greedy main

With river-waves abounding, and that earth,
Lapped in warm exhalations of the sun,
Renews her broods, and that the lusty race
Of breathing creatures bears and blooms, and that
The gliding fires of ether are alive—
What still the primal germs nowise could do,
Unless from out the infinite of space
Could come supply of matter, whence in season
They're wont whatever losses to repair.
For as the nature of breathing creatures wastes,
Losing its body, when deprived of food:
So all things have to be dissolved as soon
As matter, diverted by what means soever
From off its course, shall fail to be on hand.
Nor can the blows from outward still conserve,
On every side, whatever sum of a world
Has been united in a whole. They can
Indeed, by frequent beating, check a part,
Till others arriving may fulfil the sum;
But meanwhile often are they forced to spring
Rebounding back, and, as they spring, to yield,
Unto those elements whence a world derives,
Room and a time for flight, permitting them
To be from off the massy union borne
Free and afar. Wherefore, again, again:
Needs must there come a many for supply;
And also, that the blows themselves shall be
Unfailing ever, must there ever be
An infinite force of matter all sides round.

SEVENTEEN

Happy New Year—Really!

The Rubaiyat of Omar Khayyam

> And lately, by the Tavern Door agape,
> Came stealing through the Dusk an Angel Shape
> Bearing A Vessel on his shoulder; and
> He bid metast if it; and 'twas—the Grape!
>
> The Grape that can with Logic absolute
> The Two-and-seventy jarring Sects confute:
> The subtle Alchemist that in a Trice
> Life's leaden Metal into Gold transmute
>   — "The Rubaiyat of Omar Khayyam," verses 42-43,
>   (translated by Edward FitzGerald, first edition 1859)

It's New Year's Eve and I don't want to open a vein or crawl into a hole and pull it in after me. This is not as minor a matter as it seems. I must be maturing after all. Maturing, that is, as opposed to just getting older which is my usual Eyore-like response to December 31st.

This is the last book I plan to put into this journal, and like so many others the timing seems exactly right. Emerson had something to say about that, but then he seems to be inside my head a lot these days. Is it fate, coincidence, wish fulfillment? Probably a bit of all of the above.

The Rubaiyat, a set of four-line poems written in the mid-1400s when the Islamic world was the center of literature and science—opened the West to the fact that there may be something in the rest of the world we can learn from and aspire to.

Omar was a Sufi sheikh, or teacher who may or may not have actually been a tent maker by trade.[63] The reason we know him is that his poetry was translated by Edward FitzGerald, an Englishman, in 1859 and it became a huge cult hit.

So what's the deal? Why does it make the grade since technically Omar is the only nonwhite, European on the list? There is the question of consistency to be considered. There is also a quality issue, which I'll get to in a minute.

Much of what we know of Greek literature and philosophy was apparently kept alive by the Muslims at a time when we in the civilized West were still hiding from eclipses and burning alive anyone who dared not to observe the Sabbath. Their civilization greatly influenced ours, particularly where math and science were concerned. Even though the Spanish finally kicked them out of Europe for good in the 1400s, their legacy remains behind in a lot of medieval and Renaissance writing, even if the church didn't want to admit it.

Another reason is that it's another example of a Westerner taking work from another culture, messing with it, presenting it in a watered down but palatable form and getting famous. There is nothing more classically "white guy" than that. (Think of FitzGerald as the literary Pat Boone if it helps.)

The quality issue is of some importance, I suppose. Something tells me if these poems had been translated and published by someone other than a rich Englishman they may never have seen the light of day. People that know Persian poetry frankly don't think Omar was much of a poet, nor Fitzgerald much of a translator, but then when did THAT

---

63. Sufis had a tendency to take on other names for their writing, a tradition continued by George Sand, Mark Twain, and the Notorious B.I.G.

ever matter to the public?

Nope, what matters is that it was the first Persian poetry most of the Western public had ever been exposed to, and its impact was tremendous. All kinds of people for the first time considered looking outside their own narrow scope of literature and art.

The notion that the universe was accessible by anyone if they really wanted it was revolutionary. Emerson (him again!), Whitman and others would take that ball and run with it.

One thing about the book is there's no need to be intimidated by it whatsoever. The only reason it's a real book at all, rather than a pamphlet is it's the same 200 or so four-verse poems translated (or if the critics are to be believed, created out of whole cloth) in three different versions. Sometimes the poems are radically different, sometimes not.

On the one hand it seems a bit of a scam to create the same work of art and redo it several times. On the other hand, anyone who has sat through all three *Jurassic Park* films knows it's far from uncommon.

There are differences between them, although they are often subtle. For example in poem 12, the first version has it this way:

> "How sweet is mortal Sovranty!"—think some:
> Others—"How blest the Paradise to come!"
> Ah, take the Cash in hand and wave the Rest;
> Oh, the brave Music of a distant Drum!

Here's the same poem in Version 2, where it has mysteriously become poem 13:

> Some for the Glories of This World; and some
> Sigh for the Prophet's Paradise to come;
> Ah, take the Cash and let the Promise go,
> Nor heed the rumble of a distant Drum!

I'm no scholar, Lord knows, but in the first version, there's a sense that people either spend all their time looking forward or looking back. In the second there is a more clear call to take the money and run—to live more for today.

Quality of translation does matter in the long run, I suppose. The first translations of the great sex manual *The Kama Sutra* were done by my main man, Sir Richard Francis Burton. Apparently there were a couple of mistakes in translation that could cause serious physical harm if followed to the letter. There is talk of a class action lawsuit by a group of chiropractors.[64]

Here's what they didn't tell you in high school English class: Unless you wrote the darned poem, no one can tell you what the thing means. There are no precisely right or wrong answers, although some are more right than others.[65] This is incredibly freeing. You can read something, enjoy it (or not as the spirit moves you) and move on. THIS WILL NOT BE ON THE TEST!

Thanks to my mysterious friend on the airplane I have read more Persian poetry than just Omar. Again, the Sufis go beyond mere Islamic rhetoric to create a beautiful art form that you don't need to know more than the mere basics of Islam to appreciate. It's all about the emotional connection you should feel to the God of your choice, and that's not a bad thing.

That connection is universal. You don't have to understand Islam to get the feeling of holy intoxication. You don't have to speak in tongues to get spiritual elation. You don't have to understand Buddhism to its core to get a gut feeling of what they call samsara—although actually getting a definition of samsara can give you a twelve-pack hangover of a headache. They are all variations on the same theme.

They all feel suspiciously like the rush I feel when meditating or praying during a Taize service, a strange mix of ecumenical, Protestant, Christian chant, song and prayer. I don't know why, but it makes me feel so much better than traditional church services. It feels vaguely

---

64. Just for the record, anyone who follows the Kama Sutra to the letter is a braver human than I.
65. And some are downright wrong. See Charles Manson's rather original interpretation of Helter Skelter for the exception that proves the rule. On the other hand, I don't have the foggiest clue what the original meant. They weren't all "Hey Jude," if you know what I mean.

medieval, which is somewhat awe-inspiring in the true sense of the word, and I feel more connected to God when I am quiet than when I am in the middle of service, listening to a sermon, trying to sort history from allegory and outright whoppers and the most fervent praying that goes on is that the check I drop in the collection plate won't bounce.

It's the same sense of being plugged in to the Kosmos that the best and brightest of the Greeks, Latins, Persians, Hindus, and even Methodists have written about for centuries. It may be obvious. It may even be a little confusing, but it's definitely—most definitely— reassuring to me.

Here's a question that gnaws at me as I read Omar and the other Sufis (and stick with me because it goes from deep to silly in about 4.6 seconds). In Sufi poetry, the spiritual realm is related to wine. Intoxication is the metaphor. But there's a paradox here: Islam strictly forbids alcohol and intoxication.

- Does this mean that "the rules" of a religion don't apply when you reach a certain point?
- Is the prohibition on intoxicants in many religions a result of concern that you would settle for the false intoxicator (the high) over the legitimate (an elated, spiritual buzz) and stop growing?
- What have I been drinking?

Every culture has its intoxicants that have a part in religion. Meso-Americans had peyote and mescaline. Native Americans had tobacco. Wine is all over the Christian church, and smokables of various kinds find their way into Islam.

During the Crusades, the Assassins were a violent Muslim sect that used murder and terror for political purposes. (Relax, I'm not going there!) The most popular story is that they got their name from the hashish they would smoke before going on a raid. There's another theory that the name came from Assan, the "Old Man of the Mountain" who was their founder.

Personally, I vote for that answer for a couple of reasons. 1) Profoundly religious groups probably wouldn't break a fundamental taboo, despite the power of rationalization and; 2) I grew up in small-town Canada. I've seen enough hashish inspired behavior to know that when you use enough of it you can't stop giggling long enough to hate anybody. Furthermore, you can't hold a knife tightly enough to make a peanut butter and jelly sandwich, let alone stab someone.

All that aside, it's New Years Eve and I'm sitting in a warm house reading poems about ecstasy and joy. In forty years that's not been my MO. I dread New Year's with its constant review of the year past (just a good excuse to beat myself up for all my failures) and look ahead (like there's any reason to assume I'll get mysteriously smarter January 1?).

In my performing days, I got paid very well December 31st, which is the only reason I pulled my head out from under the blankets and ventured out among the amateur drunks and social idiots.

But I'm digging on Omar today. I'm treasuring the moment. Yes, I'm at work tomorrow. There's a ton of work to do, and the company is on shaky ground, which means some long-ass days ahead of me. But for today the sun is shining on a skiff of snow, the dog can't wait to get outside and chase a squirrel from our fence, and the wine is sweet and sings to the lips and the heart.

Here's a nice chunk of Omar. I like that bit, about transmuting life's molten lead into gold. Yeah, it can be like that on a good day.

Verse L
A Hair perhaps divides the False and True;
Yes; and a single Alif were the clue—
Could you but find it—to the Treasure-house,
And peradventure to The Master too;

LI
Whose secret Presence, through Creation's veins
Running Quicksilver-like eludes your pains;
Taking all shapes from Mah to Mahi; and

They change and perish all—but He remains;

LII

A moment guess'd—then back behind the Fold
Immerst of Darkness round the Drama roll'd
    Which, for the Pastime of Eternity,
He doth Himself contrive, enact, behold.

LIII

But if in vain, down on the stubborn floor
Of Earth, and up to Heav'n's unopening Door
    You gaze To-day, while You are You—how then
To-morrow, You when shall be You no more?

LIV

Waste not your Hour, nor in the vain pursuit
Of This and That endeavour and dispute;
    Better be jocund with the fruitful Grape
Than sadden after none, or bitter, Fruit.

LV

You know, my Friends, with what a brave Carouse
I made a Second Marriage in my house;
    Divorced old barren Reason from my Bed
And took the Daughter of the Vine to Spouse.

LVI

For "Is" and "Is-not" though with Rule and Line
And "Up" and "Down" by Logic I define,
    Of all that one should care to fathom,
Was never deep in anything but—Wine.

LVII

Ah, but my Computations, People say,
Reduced the Year to better reckoning?—Nay

'Twas only striking from the Calendar
Unborn To-morrow, and dead Yesterday.

LVIII
And lately, by the Tavern Door agape,
Came shining through the Dusk an Angel Shape
Bearing a Vessel on his Shoulder; and
He bid me taste of it; and 'twas—the Grape!

LIX
The Grape that can with Logic absolute
The Two-and-Seventy jarring Sects confute:
The sovereign Alchemist that in a trice
Life's leaden metal into Gold transmute:

Happy New Year. No, really you miserable cuss. This time I mean it.

EIGHTEEN

This Will Be on the Test

Five months and more than twenty-odd books later I think I'm done; done with my project and done with the mental heavy lifting, at least for a while. My journal is almost completely full, and Lord knows my brain is.

I think I'm overdue for a break. Time to read something with car crashes and heaving bosoms and doesn't have footnotes in Latin. It may once have been the universal language, but reading Latin, even in small chunks, makes my head hurt. It slows down my reading and, if read out loud and quickly enough, sounds like a long list of sex acts which makes me chuckle and probably isn't the intention of the authors.

I started in a white-hot frenzy, devouring these books like so much popcorn but I think I'm getting a mental tummy ache. So, it's time to take stock.

If this was all intended to get me over my mid-life crisis, I suppose on some level it worked. Don't get me wrong, I'm still feeling very forty, although I'm closer to feeling forty-one, which seems a whole lot easier to deal with somehow. My age doesn't bother me, although I'm feeling a lot like an '87 Nissan I had that seemed to know the day the warranty expired. If the warranty expired at forty that could explain more than a few things.

I know I'm easier to live with. I've been far less grumpy the last little while, and I find myself consciously stopping when I feel the steam building up. Her Serene Highness has quit hiding under the table when I come home from work, waiting to get the all clear. She's assuming it's safe until proven otherwise, and that's got to be progress, right?

I sleep a whole lot better at night, which I think speaks more to my state of mind than that the subject matter had me nodding off.[66] Sleep is never something I've done well, and even though I wake at an ungodly hour of the morning, I at least sleep until I'm done. Believe it or not, knowing that almost every one of the authors I've read was an early riser and made constructive use of that time is inspiring.

Most of this journal was written in what Kris Kristofferson likes to call the cold, grey light of dawn; when The Duchess is still sleeping and the kid hasn't started up with the cartoons and even the dog can't be bothered coming over for a belly rub. I want to get up in the morning, it's a challenge.

What was it Emerson said about turning to books only when you feel cut off from God and need inspiration? I think that's what it was. Somehow I was missing inspiration and somewhere in the stack of reading I reconnected to it.

I grin, looking back on that last paragraph. First, because I'm quoting Emerson from a position of strength this time—his work is no longer a series of disconnected quotes without context. The second, and larger reason, is because I have a whole battery of references for my thoughts. That's what Montaigne was talking about. It's why Bacon loaded his original notions with quotes from the Greeks and Latins before him. It's why Plutarch wanted everyone to know about the leaders, warriors, and losers of past generations, so they would have their own frame of reference.

I didn't know all that five months ago, or I suppose I did but it was

---

66. Okay, so I found out Horace and Erasmus are the literary equivalent of Nyquil, but they're not the norm by any stretch.

in an academic, unconnected, CSPAN/PBS kind of way. These writers are now part of my experience in the same way as the movies, TV and the other things I call on for analogies and metaphors. They are another reference point, albeit one with more credibility but less name recognition than, say, Dr. Ruth.

Does that make me smarter than I was? Maybe, depending on your definition of smart. Have I managed to cram a little more trivia into an already overcrowded attic of a noggin? Sure. (Quick, what's the name of Odysseus' wife? Too late, it's Penelope, and you don't want to pay her by the hour for her sewing.)[67] That's not why I feel smarter. I feel smarter because people I think are REALLY smart agree with me.

Some of the things they agree with I knew all along but had forgotten, lessons like "Make your choices, stick to them and see them out." Somewhere between my father's lips and my ears they'd gotten hung up in forty years of bad decisions.

The really powerful experiences were when there were amorphous ideas I couldn't quite put into words, only to find that someone had done it for me, hundreds of years before and just left them lying around in a book for me to pick up. I would feel a rush of discovery when I came across the words. A pretty good example was when Bacon talked about managing people in a way that Tom Peters and his ilk haven't articulated any better since, although they do it for more money and at a higher decibel level.

Was it worth the time I spent? Absolutely. Not only did I learn more than I expected to, but discovered I'm not alone out there; there are others (I suspect more than I know, less than I'd like to think) asking the same questions, going to the same sources and uncovering others. More than that, they're almost desperate to share, to feel a sense of connectedness to other people looking for the same kinds of answers. How did we bump into each other? Was it part of the cosmic plan, as some writers would believe? Is it the logical result of chemical and

---

67. You don't really think I'm going to tell you do you? Look it up.

atomic motion? Coincidence? Enemy action? I don't need to know, I just have to take it and be both grateful and wondering.

Did I find the answer to life's mysteries? Hell no, but I do feel a whole lot better about the little I do know. The sheer joy of Omar Khayyam, the confidence of an Emerson that we know what's right if we'd only stop long enough to listen to the directions, the Stoic acceptance of life's vagaries as something other than the whims of a cranky old God with a grudge against me personally, all spoke to me in ways that years of sermons from Sunday school on up haven't. The funny part is that the more I feel that way, the less I dread Sundays and look forward to going to the service. It's probably wrong somehow for it to have that effect on me, but it does and I'm more than okay with that.

I'm drawn more than ever to Taize services and quiet meditation. More importantly than that, I think, is the ability to be quiet. That may be the single biggest change in me over the past few months, for the first time in my life I'm able to be quiet, to just shut the #$%^ up and be. I have never been my own best friend, but at least I'm tolerable company now, even without music blaring or the TV in the background.

Am I a better husband? God I hope so. The Duchess certainly deserves my best efforts. Better father? How can I not be? The nagging question is will this feeling last? Can this be me from now on and not some temporary remission before the psychosis kicks in again?

Would I recommend this adventure to others? Hey, I don't like to recommend movies when I'm in line at Blockbuster. I know all too well that everyone's taste is different, that they come from different starting points, different traditions. I also know from painful personal experience that one person's enlightenment is another person's heresy and I try not to rock anyone's boat unnecessarily.

But yeah, I'd recommend it. I'd recommend the experience of stretching the boundaries of what you think you can tackle.

I'd recommend learning to read critically and experience the mental kick in the pants when you find a nugget worth keeping, or find out that what you read is a crock, but you can articulate why and know where to find support for your case.

And I'd recommend not making a steady diet of it. The past is the past, full of social, as well as scientific, data that is no longer relevant. I'd no sooner believe that the world is flat than that Blacks are our mental inferiors, or women too prone to hysterics to bother teaching to read. All are stated as facts by someone in those books. None are true, but does that mean nothing in them is of value? Find out for yourself.

Heck, I'm a giver; I'll get you started. For what it's worth, here is the final tally of what I read and what I thought of it. Argue with me. Track me down some day and tell me I'm wrong about Horace, or that you thought Emerson was full of it. (Say anything bad about Montaigne or Plutarch and I'll clock you one, but it's a free country, right?)

This is the complete list of the Classics Club books I waded through:

Loved It	Can take or leave it	I wouldn't read it again with your eyes
Discourses of Epictetus	Five dialogs of Plato	Selected poems of Horace
Meditations of Marcus Aurelius	*On Man in the Universe* —Aristotle	Discourses of Cicero
Essays and New Atlantis —Francis Bacon	Poems of Robert Browning	*In praise of Folly* — Erasmus
Old Goriot —Balzac	*The Iliad* — Homer	*On the Nature of Things* —Lucretius
Robinson Crusoe — Daniel Defoe	*On Politics and Education* — John Locke	*Paradise Lost* — John Milton
Essays of Ralph Waldo Emerson	*Henry Esmond* — William Thackeray	
The Odyssey — Homer	Stories by Bret Harte	
Autobiography of Benjamin Franklin	Plays by Ibsen	
Essays of Montaigne		
The Rubaiyat — Omar Khayyam		
Lives of Plutarch		
Fathers and Sons —Turgenev		

Oh, I almost forgot.
Yes, Pat, I have read them.

Bibliography

Bacon, Francis. "Of Innovation" (1625), "Of Studies" (1625). In *Francis Bacon: Essays and New Atlantis.* New York: Walter J. Black, Inc., Classics Club, 1942.

Browning, Robert. "Evelyn Hope" (1855), "Cristina" (1850), "In Three Days" (1858). In *The Selected Poems of Robert Browning.* New York: Walter J. Black, Inc., Classics Club, 1942.

——. *The Complete Poetical Works of Robert Browning,* edited by Augustine Birrell. New York: Macmillan, 1907.

Cicero [Marcus Tullius Cicero]. "Of Duty" (44 B.C.). In *Selected Works of Cicero: A New Translation,* trans. Isabelle K. and Antony E. Raubitschek and Louise R. Loomis. New York: Walter J. Black, Inc., Classics Club, 1948.

——. "To the Citizens After His Return" (n.d.). In *The Orations of Marcus Tullius Cicero,* trans. C. D. Yonge. London, 1851.

Defoe, Daniel. *Robinson Crusoe* (1719). In Daniel Defoe, *Robinson Crusoe.* New York: Walter J. Black, Inc., Classics Club, 1941.

Montaigne, Michel de. "Of Friendship" (1580), "Of the Education of Children" (1580), "Of the Force of Imagination" (1580). In *Selected Essays,* trans. Donald M. Frame. New York: Walter J. Black, Inc., Classics Club, 1943.

Emerson, Ralph Waldo. "The American Scholar" (1837), "The Divinity School Address" (1838). In *The Best of Ralph Waldo Emerson.* New York: Walter J. Black, Inc., Classics Club, 1941.

Epictetus. "Of Progress or Improvement" (n.d.). In *Epictetus:Discourses and Enchiridion,* edited by Irwin Edman. Based on trans. of Thomas Wentworth Higginson, 1896. New York: Walter J. Black, Inc., Classics Club, 1944.

Harte, Bret. "The Luck of Roaring Camp" (1867). In Bret Harte, *Selected Western Stories and Poems.* New York: Walter J. Black, Inc., Classics Club, 1932.

——. "The Poet of Sierra Flat." *The Atlantic Monthly* 28, no. 165 (July 1871).

Homer. *The Iliad* (n.d.). In *The Iliad of Homer,* trans. Samuel Butler, 1898. Edited by Louise R. Loomis. New York: Walter J. Black, Inc., Classics Club, 1942.

——. *The Odyssey* (n.d.). In *The Odyssey of Homer,* trans. Samuel Butler, 1900. Edited by Louise R. Loomis. New York: Walter J. Black, Inc. Classics Club, 1944.

Ibsen, Henrik. *The Master Builder* (1892). In Henrik Ibsen, *Seven Plays.* New York: Walter J. Black, Inc., Classics Club, 1942.

——. *An Enemy of the People* (1882). In Henrik Ibsen, *An Enemy of the People,* trans. R. Farquharson Sharp, 1972. Project Gutenberg; gutenberg.net; Internet.

Khayyam, Omar. "The Rubaiyat" (c. 15th cent.) In *The Rubaiyat of Omar Khayyam,* trans. Edward Fitzgerald, version 1, 1859; version 2, 1868. New York: Walter J. Black, Inc., Classics Club, 1942.

Locke, John. "Second Treatise of Government" (1690). In *John Locke: On Politics and Education.* New York: Walter J. Black, Inc., Classics Club, 1947.

Lucretius [Titus Lucretius Carus]. *On the Nature of Things* (50 B.C.E.). In *On the Nature of Things,* trans. Charles E. Bennett. New York: Walter J. Black, Inc., Classics Club, 1945.

——. *The Nature of Things,* "Book 2," (1914), trans. William Ellery Leonard, 1898. classics.mit.edu/Carus/nature_things.html; Internet.

Milton, John. *Paradise Lost,* third ed. (1667). In *Paradise Lost and Other Poems: John Milton,* edited by Maurice Kelley. New York: Walter J. Black, Inc., Classics Club, 1943.

Plutarch [Mestrius Plutarchus]. "Pericles" (n.d.), "Comparison of Demosthenes and Cicero" (n.d.). In *Plutarch: Selected Lives and Essays,* translated from the Greek by Louise Ropes Loomis. New York: Walter J. Black, Inc., Classics Club, 1951.

——. *Lives of Plutarch,* trans. Dryden-Clough, 1898. classics.mit.edu/Browse/browse-Plutarch.html; Internet.

Richardson, Robert D. *Emerson: The Mind on Fire.* Los Angeles, California: University of California Press, 1995.

Ruiz, Miguel. *The Four Agreements.* San Rafael, California: Amber-Allen Publishing, 1997.

Shah, Indries. *The Sufis.* New York: Doubleday, 1964.